Father God Zeus

Revised Edition

By Rita Jean Moran

Contents

Chapter 1 7
    Zeus 7

Chapter 2 12
    Zagreus-Dionysus-Osiris 12

Chapter 3 39
    The Olympians and Ariadne-Isis 39

Chapter 4 45
    The Stories of the Greek Gods and Goddesses 45

Chapter 5 53
    Manetho Timeline, Red Horn, White Buffalo Woman, ... 53
    and Red-Haired Giants 53

Chapter 6 72
    Nordic Mythology, Travels to Vinland, Celtic Mythology, Travels to America 72

Chapter 7 89
    Egyptian Mythology 89

Chapter 8 95
    Hinduism 95

Chapter 9 101
    Chinese and Japanese Mythology 101

Chapter 10 104
    African Pantheons 104

Chapter 11 106
    Polynesian and Aborigine Pantheons 106

Chapter 12 115
    Nag Hammadi Library, Dead Sea Scrolls, and Book of Enoch 115

Chapter 13 121
Forbidden Texts 121

Chapter 14 129
    Giants and Little People Everywhere 129

Chapter 15 133

Mounds, Effigies, Megalithic Structures, ...133

  Human Origins, and World Catastrophies 133

Chapter 16 135

  Modern Religion, Alice Bailey, and Mystery Cults..135

Copyright © 2013

Printed in the United States of America

No one Knows You
(Dedicated to Zeus)

I took a path unknown,
What I found has my mind blown,
A tale no one knows,
A tale of ancient foes.

No one knows you,
No one knows you,
Your story is lost in time,
Hidden in ancient verses and rhyme.

Your family changed the world,
You traveled the whole globe,
It was such a bad scene,
You got through it, it was so mean.

No one knows you,
No one knows you,
Your story is lost in time,
Hidden in ancient verses and rhyme.

They took your son away,
What they did, I don't want to say,
In the end they all paid,
Your body, in the fire they layed.

No one knows you,

No one knows you,
Your story is lost in time,
Hidden in ancient verses and rhyme.

Chapter 1

Zeus

The Queen of Sheba, from a 15th-century manuscript now at Staats - und Universitätsbibliothek Gottingen – public domain

I've been researching ancient mythology and other subjects for a very long time. At the age of ten, I realized something wasn't quite right about the history they were teaching in school. When I heard that the cultures of ancient Mesoamerica and ancient Egypt were not in contact, I knew that there was something wrong about that theory. I could tell there were too many similarities in cultures for the two societies to have been separated. The commonalities in pyramid construction, royalty, rites of the dead, and pantheons were too strong for it to just be a coincidence. As I got older, I worked a mainstream job, but my interest in ancient mythology and ancient people never went away. In fact it's a passion that has lasted for over thirty years and continues, today. But the biggest find of a lifetime, had to be the gradual realization that all mythologies around the world are based on the same group of genetically related people that existed thousands of years ago. The proof exists not only in the artifacts that remain, but in a group of ancient writings from Greek, Roman, Nordic, Celtic, Mayan, Aztec, and Egyptian writers. I found a story that no one has told in a very long time. It is the story of a man that went by many names and the trials that he and his family went through. It is the story of the God we call, Zeus.

    His story is salacious to some degree. Tales of patricide, cannibalism, incest, war, murder, lust, jealousy, betrayal, and more weave their way all through his life. But tales of redemption, global journeys, love, higher ideals, knowledge, education, honor, and survival also weave their way into his life. The story of Zeus and his family is the story the world should know. If you know a little bit about mythology of any culture, you already know some of the story. But the world does not fully understand him or what he and his family did for the world. He did not like what the humans and fellow giants were doing and he wanted to replace the whole human race with a new race. That race would be a race from his own bloodline and he almost did just that. Most Europeans are from his bloodline and they don't even know it. They are truly the children of this God. Let me tell you the details of his life.

    He is known as the Greek Zeus, Roman Jupiter, Jewish Jupiter Sabazius, Sumerian Enki and Ea, Celtic Daghda and Cernunnos, Nordic Odin, Egyptian Geb and Ammon, Chinese Jade Emperor, Japanese Izanagi, Mayan Itzamna, Aztec Huitzlipotchli, Incan Inti and Viracocha, Gnostic Sabaoth, Hindu Indra, Shiva, Brahma, and Vishnu, Hare in Ho-Chunk legends, and many other names I have yet to discover. I determined this based on the consistent story of the murdered son of this God, comparative mythology, and the writings from ancient Greek, Roman, Nordic, Celtic, Mayan, Aztec, and Egyptian scholars.

His childhood started out as a violent one. His father was Cronus, a god known for murdering and castrating his father to take over the throne and rule the world. A prophecy was given to Cronus that a son born to him would overthrow him one day as he had overthrown his father. Because of this prophecy, it is said that Cronus swallowed all of his children, but one. His wife Rhea tricked Cronus into swallowing a rock, swaddled in clothing. Rhea hid baby Zeus in a cave known as Mt. Ida in Crete where he was given goat's milk and honey and raised by the nymph named, Adamanthea. He was guarded by the Kouretes, who were soldiers that would clash their swords together when baby Zeus cried, to hide his cries from his enemies.

Zeus grew up and learned many things from his mother Rhea and her followers. He learned all about agriculture, love, nature, and life from his mother and her followers. He became a strong warrior with a love for nature and knowledge of agriculture and farming. Food was plentiful under the guidance of Rhea.

Rhea was the mother goddess. She had her own followers. Her mysteries included agriculture, sex and love, music and trance, medicinal plants, shamanism, and ability to see the future. She taught her children and grandchildren all of her ways. Rhea had six children by Cronus including: Hades, Poseidon, Zeus, Hestia, Hera, and Demeter. Some say Hades was another name for Zeus. There are variations in the myths. Rhea lived in what is now known as Turkey. Her followers wore Phyrgian caps. This cap represented freedom and liberty. The cap is similar to the top part of a witch's hat. The hat is conical in shape, which is quite interesting in itself.

Zeus grew up and is said to have freed his brothers and sisters. He was said to have had a strong sexual appetite. He mated with several female Titans before he impregnated his youngest sister, Hera. With Hera, he had six children (2 boys and 4 girls). But that was not enough for Zeus. He seduced many more female Titans and human women. He abducted Europa and impregnated her. He even abducted and impregnated his own daughter, Persephone, as some myths say. It is not clear, if he knew that this was his daughter. It was with Persephone, that Zagreus was born.

Zagreus was his favorite son. He wanted Zagreus to inherit his kingdom. Zeus was a King of Crete, but he was also the king of the world since he had dethroned his father. Zeus had many enemies amongst the Titans. His wife Hera, was jealous of all of his concubines and illegitimate children. It is said that she plotted with the Titans to kill Zagreus.

When Zeus was away, several Titans slipped in past the guards of Zagreus and tricked him with a mirror and toys. They slew the child with knives, divided up his body, and ate it. It is said that Athena was able to recover the heart of Zagreus and give it back to Zeus.

Zeus was enraged when he came home and found the slain Zagreus. He vowed revenge and it is said he traced down the Titans who did this and tortured them to death. He hung his wife, Hera, up in the sky for her part in it. It was her son who had to rescue her, later.

Zeus took the heart and made a drink potion with it. He drank it, believing it had the soul of Zagreus in it and that he could transfer this soul into another child. He impregnated Semele and believed he transferred the soul of Zagreus into her child. This child was born and was named Dionysus. Dionysus was to inherit his father's kingdom and so he did as the Pharaoh, Osiris.

To protect Dionysus, Zeus, had his mother Rhea, raise him as a girl. She dressed him up as a girl and taught him everything she knew about agriculture, medicine, war, and love. He escaped the angry eyes of Hera and his enemies, the Titans, and grew up into a man. His father told him to go and civilize the world and so he did.

After Osiris-Dionysus civilized the world with the help of his father, brothers, sisters, and an army, he came back to Egypt where he was tricked by Set and was subsequently murdered by a group of conspirators. The son of Osiris, Horus, avenged his father's death and the kingdom of Egypt was divided into lower and upper Egypt.

Picking up the story of Ragnarok, from Nordic traditions, Odin-Zeus, is murdered by the son of Loki, the Fenrir wolf. One of the sons (relatives) of Odin-Zeus, Vidar, avenges his death and murders the Fenrir Wolf (some say Vidar was the Greek Aeneus who was the founder of the ancient Romans and he was the son of Aphrodite). The identity of Loki is Set, Prometheus, the Trickster, Lucifer, Satan, sometimes the Devil, and many other names. Prometheus and his bloodline became the enemy of Zeus and his bloodline through trickery, betrayal, and murder. Prometheus claimed to be a benefactor of humans, but in the end, he lusted for power and to have his descendants be the ruling bloodline on the planet. Perhaps this battle took place after the murder of Osiris. It was said that three of Loki's children were destroyed, but Deucalion was also the son of Prometheus-Loki and he does not appear to have been killed.

The bloodline of Zeus and the Cronides survived and traveled the world. It exists all over Europe, America , and probably in the ancient royalty of the MesoAmericas. I do not believe the people who sit on the thrones of the world today are the direct descendants of the Cronides. The ancient Hyksos are said to be the ancestors of the Semite and their god was Set. It is interesting to note the attempted exterminations of people including the Irish, Germanic Celts, the Native Americans, and all legitimate royalty. Is it any wonder, the world is in the state it is today?

There are still tribes in Papua New Guinea and the Amazon who practice cannibalism, but for the most part, that practice has been exterminated and the giants who practiced it were exterminated as well. The Father's Prayer tells you he gave you your daily bread through his sons and daughters and his bloodline.

Our father who art in heaven,
Hallowed be thy name,
Thy kingdom come, thy will be done,
Give us this day our daily bread and forgive us our
trespasses as we forgive those who trespass against us.
For yours is the kingdom now and forever…Amen (Ammon-Zeus).

Chapter 2

Zagreus-Dionysus-Osiris

A legend was written about in many books of the ancient Greeks, Romans, and Egyptians. It is also spoken about in the ancient stories of the Americas and oral traditions of mythologies across Europe and the rest of the world. It is the story of Osiris-Dionysus. It is the story of the travels of Dionysus as he, his family, and a private army traveled the world to civilize it and teach sacred mysteries to all of the people after the entire world had sunken into cannibalism and savagery. He is the one responsible for re-building civilization after a major war. He is the one who is behind the *Mythological Unification Theory* (see Mythological Unification Theory (M.U.T.) by Rita Jean Moran). He was written about by Plutarch, Diordorus Siculus, Nonnos, Manetho, and many others.

As I wrote in the book, M.U.T., Dionysus went by many names in various cultures around the world. Here is a short list of many of his names:

God/ Goddess Name	Symbols	Sacred Animals	Skills	Spouse/ Consort	Parent	Death
Dionysus (Greek)	Alcohol, Grapes	Goat, Bull	Farming, Wine making		Zeus	Killed by Titans
Bacchus (Roman)	Alcohol, Grape	Goat, Bull	Farming, Wine making		Jupiter	Killed by Titans
Dumuzi or Tammuz	Shepherd	Bull, Goat	Agriculture	Ishtar/ Inanna	Ea and Damkin	Killed by Group of

(Mesopotamin)					a	other gods
Baal (Canaanite)	Phrygian Cap	Bull	Son of El, Smiting Pose, Osiris Cap without feathers	Ishtar		
Osiris (Egyptian)	Crook and Flail	Lion	God of Fertility, Agriculture, the Good Shepherd	Isis	Nuit and Geb Horus	Killed by Set
Serapis (Roman)						
Queztlcoatl, Kulkucan (MesoAmerican)	Feathered Serpent		Teacher			
Balder (Nordic)	Holly leaf killed him		Son		Odin and Frigga	Killed by trickery with a holly dart
Óengus (Celtic)	Warrior	Warrior		Caer Ibormeith	Daghda and Boann	
Niu Lang (Chinese)	Cows		Cow Herder	Weaver Maiden		
Lono (Polynesian)	Vegetation		God of Agriculture and fertility			
Tsukuyomi	Moon God	The		Amaterasu	Izanagi	Killed by

(Japanese)		Moon God,				Susano
Sabazious (Greek)	Sacred Hand with symbols					

Diodorus Siculus was a Greek scholar who lived in Sicily from 80 BC to 20 BC. He devoted thirty years of his life to research the history of the world and write about it in his books entitled, *Library of History*. He traveled to Egypt to learn from the scholars there. He wrote forty books and twenty of them survive, today. Pieces of the other twenty books can be found in the works of other scholars of the time. Here is what he wrote about the god and the goddess.

Now the men of Egypt, they say, when ages ago they came into existence, as they looked up at the firmament and were struck with both awe and wonder at the nature of the universe, conceived that two gods were both eternal and first, namely, the sun and the moon, whom they called respectively Osiris and Isis, these appellations having in each case been based upon a certain meaning in them. For when the names are translated into Greek Osiris means "many-eyed," and properly so; for in shedding his rays in every direction he surveys with many eyes, as it were, all land and sea. And the words of the poet are also in agreement with this conception when he says:

The sun, who sees all things and hears all things.

And of the ancient Greek writers of mythology some give to Osiris the name Dionysus or, with a slight change in form, Sirius. One of them, Eumolpus, in his Bacchic Hymn speaks of Our Dionysus, shining like a star, with fiery eye in ev'ry ray;
While Orpheus says:

And this is why men call him Shining One and Dionysus.

Some say that Osiris is also represented with the cloak of fawn-skin about his shoulders as imitating the sky spangled with the stars. As for Isis, when translated the word means "ancient," the name having been given her because her birth was from everlasting and ancient. And they put horns on her head both because of the appearance

which she has to the eye when the moon is crescent-shaped, and because among the Egyptians a cow is held sacred to her.

These two gods, they hold, regulate the entire universe, giving both nourishment and increase to all things by means of a system of three seasons which complete the full cycle through an unobservable movement, these being spring and summer and winter; and these seasons, though in nature most opposed to one another, complete the cycle of the year to fullest harmony. Moreover, practically all the physical mater which is essential to the generation of all things is furnished by these gods, the sun contributing the fiery element and the spirit, the moon the wet and the dry, and both together the air; and it is through those elements that all things are engendered and nourished. And so it is out of the sun and moon that the whole physical body of the universe is made complete; and as for the five parts just named of these bodies-the spirit, the fire, the dry as well as the wet, and, lastly, the air-like-just as in the case of a man we enumerate head and hands and feet and the other parts, so in the same way the body of the universe is composed in its entirety of these parts.

Each of the parts they regard as a god and to each of them the first men in Egypt to use articulate speech gave a distinct name appropriate in its nature. Now the spirit they called, as we translate their expression, Zeus, and since he was the source of the spirit of life in animals they considered him to be in a sense the father of all things. And they say that the most renowned of the Greek poets also agrees with this when he speaks of this god as the father of men and of gods.

The fire they called Hephaestus, as it is translated, holding him to be a great god and one who contributes much both to the birth and full development of all things. The earth, again, they looked upon as a kind of vessel which holds all growing things and so gave it the name "mother"; and in like manner the Greeks also call it Demeter, the word having been slightly changed in the course of time; for in olden times they called her Ge Meter (Earth Mother), to which Orpheus bears witness when he speaks of

Earth the Mother of all, Demeter giver of wealth.

And the wet according to them, was called by the men of old Oceane, which, when translated, means Fostering-mother, though some of the Greeks have taken it to be Oceanus, in connection with whom the poet also speaks of

Oceanus source of gods and mother Tethys.

For the Egyptians consider Oceanus to be their river Nile, on which also their gods were born; since, they say, Egypt is the only country in the whole inhabited world where there are many cities which were founded by the first gods, such as Zeus, Helius, Hermes, Apollo Pan, Eileithyai, and many more.

The air, they say, they called Athena was the name is translated, and they considered her to be a daughter of Zeus and conceived of her as a virgin, because of the fact that the air is by its nature uncorrupted and occupies the highest part of the entire universe; for the latter reason also the myth arose that she was born from the head of Zeus.

Another name given her was Tritogeneia (Thrice-born), because her nature changes three times in the course of the year, in the spring, summer, and winter. They add that she is also called Glaucopia (Blue-eyed), not because she has blue eyes, as some Greeks have held- a silly explanation, indeed-but because the air has a bluish cast.

These five deities, they say, visit all the inhabited world, revealing themselves to men in the form of sacred animals, and at times even appearing in the guise of men or in other shapes; nor is this a fabulous thing, but possible, if these are in very truth the gods who give life to all things. And also the poet, who visited Egypt and became acquainted with such accounts as these from the lips of the priests, in some place in his writings sets forth as actual fact that has been said:

The gods, in strangers form from alien lands, Frequent the cities of men in ev'ry guise, Observing their insolence and lawful ways.

Now so far as the celestial gods are concerned whose genesis is from eternity, this is the account given by the Egyptians.

And besides these there are other gods, they say, who were terrestrial, having once been mortals, but who, by reason of their sagacity and the good services which they rendered to all men, attained immortality, some of them having been kings in Egypt. Their names, when translated, are in some cases the same as those of the celestial gods, while others have a distinct appellation, such as Helios, Cronus, and Rhea, and also the Zeus who is called Ammon by some, and besides these Hera and Hephaestus, also Hestia, and finally, Hermes. Helius was the first king of the Egyptians, his name being the same as that of the heavenly star. Some of the priests, however, say that Hephaestus was their first king, since he was the discover of fire and received the rule because of this service to mankind; for once, when a tree on the mountains had been struck by lightning and the forest nearby was ablaze, Hephaestus went up to it, for it was winter-time, and greatly enjoyed the heat; as the fire died down he kept adding fuel to it, and while keeping the fire going in this way he invited the rest of mankind to enjoy the advantage which came from it. Then Cronus became the ruler, and upon marrying his sister Rhea he beget Osiris and Isis, according to some writers of mythology, but, according to the majority, Zeus and Hera, whose high achievements gave them dominion over the entire universe. From these last were sprung five gods, one born on each of the five days which the Egyptians intercalate; the names of these children were Osiris and Isis, and also Typhon, Apollo, and Aphrodite; and Osiris when translated is Dionysus, and Isis is more similar to Demeter than to any other goddess; and after Osiris married Isis and succeeded to the kingship he did many things of service to the social life of man.

    Osiris was the first, they record, to make mankind give up cannibalism; for after Isis had discovered the fruit of both wheat and barley which grew wild over the land along with the other plants but was still unknown to man, and Osiris had also devised the cultivation of these fruits, all men were glad to change their food, both because of the pleasing nature of the newly-discovered grains and because it seemed to their advantage to refrain from their butchery of one another. As proof of the discovery of these fruits they offer the following ancient custom which they still observe: Even yet at harvest time the people make a dedication of the first heads of the grain to be cut, and standing beside the sheaf beat themselves and call upon Isis, by this act rendering honour to the goddess for the fruits which she discovered, at the season when she first did this. Moreover in some cities, during the Festival of Isis as well, stalks of wheat and barley are carried among the other objects in the procession, as a memorial of what the goddess so ingeniously discovered at the beginning. Isis also established laws, they say, in accordance with which the people regularly dispense justice to one another and are led to refrain through fear of punishment from illegal violence and insolence; and it is for this reason also that the early Greeks gave Demeter the name Thesmophorus acknowledging in this way that she had first established their laws.

Osiris, they say, founded in the Egyptian Thebaid a city with a hundred gates, which the men of his day named after his mother, though later generations called it Diospolis, and some named it Thebes. There is no agreement, however, as to when this city was founded, not only among the historians, but even among the priests of Egypt themselves; for many writers say that Thebes was not founded by Osiris, but many years later by a certain king of whom we shall give a detailed account in connection with his period. Osiris, they add, also built a temple to his parents, Zeus and Hera, which was famous both for its size and the costliness in general, and two golden chapels to Zeus, the larger one to him as god of heaven, the smaller one to him as former king and father of the Egyptians, in which role he is called by some Ammon. He also made golden chapels for the rest of the gods mentioned above, allotting honours to each of them and appointing priests to have charge over these. Special esteem at the court of Osiris and Isis was also accorded to those who should invent any of the arts or devise any useful process; consequently, since copper and gold mines had been discovered in the Thebaid, they fashioned implements with which they killed the wild beasts and worked the soil, and thus in eager rivalry brought the country under cultivation, and they made images of the gods and magnificent golden chapels for their worship.

Osiris, they say, was also interested in agriculture and was reared in Nyssa, a city of Arabia Felix near Egypt near Egypt, being a son of Zeus; and the name which he bears among the Greeks is derived both from his father and from the birthplace, since he is called Dionysus. Mention is also made of Nyssa by the poet in his Hymns to the effect that it was in the vicinity of Egypt when he says:

> There is a certain Nysa, mountain high, With forests thick in Phoenice afar, Close to Aegyptus' streams.

And the discovery of the vine, they say, was made by him near Nysa, and that, having further devised the proper treatment of its fruit, he was the first to drink wine and taught mankind at large the culture of the vine and the use of wine, as well as the way to harvest the grape and to store the wine. The one most highly honoured by him was Hermes, who was endowed with unusual ingenuity for devising things capable of improving the social life of man.

It was by Hermes, for instance, according to them, that the common language of mankind was first further articulated, and that many objects which were still nameless received an appellation, that the alphabet was invented, and that ordinances regarding the honours and offerings due to the gods were duly established; he was the first also to observe the orderly arrangement of the stars and the harmony of the musical sounds and their nature, to establish a wrestling school, and to give thought to the rhythmical movement of the human body and its proper development. He also made a lyre and gave it three strings, imitating the seasons of the year; for he adopted three tones, a high, a low, and a medium; the high from the summer, the low from the winter, and the medium from the spring. The Greeks also were taught by him how to expound their thoughts, and it was for this reason that he was given the name Hermes. In a word, Osiris, taking him for his priestly scribe, communicated with him on every matter and used his counsel above that of all others. The olive tree also, they claim was his discovery, not Athena's as Greeks say.

Of Osiris they say that, being of a beneficent turn of mind, and eager for glory, he gathered together a great army, with the intention of visiting all the inhabited earth and teaching the race of men how to cultivate the vine and sow wheat and barley; for he supposed that if he made men give up their savagery and adopt a gentle manner of life he would receive immortal honours because of the magnitude of his benefactions. And this did in fact take place, since not only the men of his time who received this gift, but all succeeding generations as well, because of the delight which they take in the foods which were discovered, have honoured those who introduced them as gods most illustrious.

Now after Osiris had established the affairs of Egypt and turned the supreme power over to Isis his wife, they say that he placed Hermes at her side as counsellor because his prudence raised him above the king's other friends, and as general of all the land under his sway he left Heracles, who was both his kinsman and renowned for his valour and physical strength, while as governors he appointed Bursiris over those parts of Egypt which lie

towards Phoenicia and border upon the sea and Antaeus over those adjoining Ethiopia and Libya; then he himself left Egypt with his army to make his campaign, taking his company also his brother, whom the Greeks call Apollo. And it was Apollo, they say, who discovered the laurel, a garland of which all men place about the head of this god above all others. The discovery of ivy is also attributed to Osiris and made sacred to this god, just as the Greeks also do in the case of Dionysus and in the Egyptians language, they say, the ivy is called the "plant of Osiris" and for purposes of dedication is preferred to the vine, since the latter sheds its leaves while the former ever remains green; the same rule, moreover, the ancients have followed in the case of other plants also which are perennially green, ascribing, for instance, the myrtle to Aphrodite an the laurel to Apollo.

Now Osiris was accompanied on his campaign, as the Egyptian account goes, by his two sons Anubis and Macedon, who were distinguished for their valour. Both of them carried the most notable accoutrements of war, taken from certain animals whose character was not unlike the boldness of the men, Anubis wearing a dog's skin and Macedon the fore-parts of a wolf; and it is for this reason that these animals are held in honour among the Egyptians. He also took Pan along on his campaign, who is held in special honour by the Egyptians; for the inhabitants of the land have not only set up statues of him at very temple but have also named a city after him in the Thebaid, called by the native Chemmo, which when translated means City of Pan.[1]

The story continues on with Osiris visiting Ethiopia, India, and other parts of the world. It was said he was not warlike and the people received him well. But in Thrace he slew Lycurgus, thinking of the barbarians, who opposed his undertakings, and Maron, who was now old, he left there to supervise the culture.

Finally, Osiris in this way visited all the inhabited world and advanced community life by the introduction of the fruits which are most easily cultivated. And if any country did not admit of the growing of the vine he introduced the drink prepared from barley, which is little inferior to wine in aroma and in strength. On his return to Egypt he

---

[1] Diodorus Siculus, *The Library of History Volume 1*, pages 37-57.

brought with him the very greatest presents from every quarter and by reason of the magnitude of his benefactions received the gift of immortality with the approval of all men and honour equal to that offered to the gods of heaven. After this he passed from the midst of men into the company of the gods and received from Isis and Hermes sacrifices and every other highest honour. These also instituted rites for him and introduced many things of a mystic nature, magnifying in the way the power of the god.[2]

Although the priests of Osiris had from the earliest times received the account of his death as a matter not to be divulged, in the course of years it came about that through some of their number this hidden knowledge was published to the many. This is the story as they give it: When Osiris was ruling over Egypt as its lawful king, he was murdered by his brother Typhon, a violent and impious man; Typhon then divided the body of the slain man into twenty-six pieces and gave one portion to each of the band of murderers, since he wanted all of them to share in the pollution and felt that in this way he would have in them steadfast supporters and defenders of his rule. But, Isis the sister and wife of Osiris, avenged his murder with the aid of her son Horus, and after slaying Typhon and his accomplices became queen over Egypt. The struggle between them took place on the banks of the Nile near the village now known as Antaeus, which, they say, lies on the Arabian side of the river and derives its name from that Antaeus, a contemporary of Osiris, who was punished by Heracles. Now Isis recovered all the pieces of the body except the privates, and wishing that the burial-place of her husband should remain secret and yet be honoured by all the inhabitants of Egypt, she fulfilled her purpose in somewhat the following manner. Over each piece of the body, as the account goes, she fashioned out of spices and wax a human figure about the size of Osiris; then summoning the priests group by group, she required all of them an oath that they would reveal to no one the trust which she was going to confide to them, and taking each group of them part privately she said that she was consigning to them alone the burial of the body, and after reminding them of the benefactions of Osiris she exhorted them to bury his body in their own district and pay honours to him as to a god, and to consecrate to him also some one that they might choose of the animals native to their district, pay it while living the honours which they had

---

[2] Diodorus Siculus, *The Library of History Volume 1*, page 65.

formally rendered to Osiris, and upon its death accord it the same kind of funeral as they had given to him. And since Isis wished to induce the priests to render these honours by the incentive of their own profit also, she gave them the third part of the country to defray the cost of the worship and service of the gods. And the priests, it is said, being mindful of the benefactions of Osiris and eager to please the queen who was petitioning them, and incited as well by their own profit, did everything just as Isis had suggested. It is for this reason that even to this day each group of priests supposes that Osiris lies buried in their district, pays honours to the animals which were originally consecrated to him, and when these die, renews in the funeral rites for them the mourning of Osiris. The consecration to Osiris however, of the sacred bulls which are given the names Apis and Mnevis, and the worship of them as gods we introduced generally among all the Egyptians, since these animals and, more than any others, rendered aid to those who discovered the fruit of the grain, in connection with both the sowing of the seed and with every agricultural labour from which mankind profits.

Isis, they say, after the death of Osiris took a vow never to marry another man, and passed the remainder of her life reigning over the land with complete respect for the law and surpassing all sovereigns in benefactions to her subjects. And like her husband she also, when she passed from among men, received immortal honours and was buried near Memphis, where her shrine is pointed out to this day in the temple-area of Hephaestus. According to some writers, however, the bodies of these two gods rest, not in Memphis, but on the border between Egypt and Ethiopia, on the island in the Nile which lies near the city which is called Philae, but is referred to because of this burial as the Holy Field. …

Consequently the Greeks too, inasmuch as they received from Egypt the celebrations of the orgies and the festivals connected with Dionysus, honour this member in both the mysteries and the initiatory rites and sacrifices of this god, giving it the name "phallus."

The number of years from Osiris and Isis, they say, to the reign of Alexander, who founded the city which bears his name in Egypt, is over ten thousand but according to other writers, a little less than twenty-three thousand. And those who say that the god was born of Semele and Zeus in Boeotia Thebes are, according to the priests, simply inventing the tale.[3]

As for Isis, the Egyptians say that she was the discoverer of many health-giving drugs and was greatly versed in the science of healing; consequently, now that she has attained immortality, she finds her greatest delights in the healing of mankind and gives aid to their sleep to those how call upon her, plainly manifesting both her very presence and her beneficence towards men who ask for help.

Furthermore, she discovered also the drug which gives immortality, by means of which she not only raised from the dead her son Horus, who had been the object of plots on the part of the Titans and had been found dead under the water, giving him his soul again, but also made him immortal…[4]

And, as their legends say, the most ancient of the gods ruled more than twelve hundred years and the later ones not less than three hundred. But since this great number of years surpasses belief, some men would maintain that in early times, before the movement of the sun had as yet been recognized, it was customary to reckon the year by the lunar cycle.[5]

Furthermore, the Egyptians relate in their myths that in the time of Isis there were certain creatures of many bodies, who were called by the Greeks Giants, but by themselves…., these being the men who are represented on their temples in monstrous form and as being cudgelled by Osiris…..[6]

---

[3]Diodorus Siculus, *The Library of History Volume 1*, pages 65-73.

[4]Diodorus Siculus, *The Library of History Volume 1*, pages 81-82.

[5] Diodorus Siculus, *The Library of History Volume 1*, page 83.
[6]Diodorus Siculus, *The Library of History Volume 1*, page 85.

The writings of Nonnos are very interesting as well. Nonnos was a Greek scholar who flourished in Egypt during the 5th century. He wrote an epic poem called, The Dionysiaca. This epic poem describes the birth of Dionysus, his youth among the Corybantes and Satyrs and his upbringing by his grandmother Rhea, his invention of wine in honour of the death of childhood friend named Ampelos, his war campaign in India, his spreading of his rites and wine cult, his loves and not so ethical love conquests, and much more. He dressed in purple, wore snakes in his hair or a laurel wreath, wore a woman's girdle, and used a Thyrsus as a weapon. He was considered to be an effeminate male god and his army consisted of women and satyrs and trained lions and panthers who did the killing. Here are a few passages from The Dionysiaca:

O mighty Dionysus! Your father bids you destroy the race of Indians, untaught of piety. Come lift the thyrsus of battle in our hands and earn heaven by your deeds.[7]

Oft he would show himself like a young girl in saffron robes and take on the feigned shape of a woman; to mislead the mind of spiteful Hera, he molded his lips to speak in a girlish voice, tied a scented veil on his hair. He put on all a woman's manycolored garments: fastened a maiden's vest about his chest and the firm circle of his bosom, and fitted a purple girdle over his hips like a band of maidenhood.

But his guile was useless. Hera, who turns her all-seeing eye to every place saw from on high the ever-changing shape of Lyaios, and knew all. Then she was angry with the guardians of Bromios.[8]

He only tied his loose tresses with serpent-knots, a grim garland for his head; instead of fine wrought greaves, from ankle to thigh he wore purple buskins on his silvery feet.[9]

---

[7] Nonnos, *Dionysica Books 1-xv*, page 429.
[8] Nonnos, *Dionysica Books 1-xv*, pages 484-485.
[9] Nonnos, *Dionysica Books 1-xv*, page 485.

> In the morning, the god went forth to war, driving before him the violence of the black men, that he might free the neck of the Lydians and those who dwelt in Phyrgia and Ascania from the yoke of cruel tyranny.
>
> But swiftshoe Hera, likening herself to an Indian, the curly-headed Melaneus, warned Astraeis, that spear shakingcaptain of men, not to uplift the thyrsus nor to heed the yell of drunken Satyrs, but to raise war to the death against Dionysos.
>
> You that array a crowd of women against my armies, fight if you can with your womanish thyrsus! Play the champion if you can! And if you delight the heart of all mankind, all conquering, now charm one only whom nothing can charm- Orontes!
>
> Lord Bacchus was angry when he heard him, and with a vine cluster he tapped him gently on the chest. This tap of an insignificant vine grown bloom split his breast piece. The god's pike did not touch the protected flesh, did not scratch his body; but the coat of mail broke and fell with a heavy clang-Orontes was naked!
>
> Tribes of leopards and wild packs of lions and hunting-dogs took turns in guarding Dionysos in the wilderness with sleepless eyes; all night they kept vigil in the mountain forest, that no assault of black Indians might approach him. Long lines of torches flashed up to Olympus, the lights of the dancing Bacchants which had no rest.[10]

There was an elder Dionysus mentioned that Dionysus was named after who was Indian. But there was a toddler Dionysus who was called Zagreus, and the child was slain by the Titans. Zagreus was the child of Zeus and his daughter, Persephone. Dionysus-Osiris was the reincarnation of Zagreus.

> By the fierce resentment of implacable Hera, the Titans cunningly smeared their round faces with disguising chalk, and while he contemplated his changeling countenance reflected in a mirror they destroyed him with an infernal knife. There where his limbs had been cut piecemeal by the titan steel, the end of his life was the beginning of a new life as Dionysos. He appeared in another shape, and changed into many forms: now young like crafty Cronides shaking the aegis-cape, now as an

---

[10] Nonnos, *Dionysiaca I Books 1-XV*, pages 489- 501

ancient Cronos heavy- kneed, pouring rain. Sometimes he was a curiously formed baby, sometimes like a mad youth with the flower of the first down marking his rounded chin with black.[11]

- Nonnos, *Dionysiaca Volume 1*, page 227.

Drinking Bacchus (1623) Guido Reni. - public domain

After the first Dionysos had been slaughtered, Father Zeus learnt the trick of the mirror with its reflected image. He attacked the mother of the Titans with avenging brand, and shut up the murderers of horned Dionysos within the gate of Tartaros: the trees blazed, the hair of suffering Earth was scorched with heat. He kindled the bolts, the Assyrian waves set afire the neighbouring Caspian Sea and the Indian mountains, the Red Sea rolled billows of flame and warned Arabian Nereus The opposite West also fiery Zeus blasted with his thunderbolt in love for his child; and under the foot of Zephyros the western brine half-burnt spat out a shining stream; the northern ridges-even the surface of the frozen Northern Sea bubbled

---

[11] Nonnos, *Dionysiaca Volume 1*, page 227.

> and burned: under the clime of snowy Aigoceros the Southern corner boiled with hotter sparks.[12]

- Nonnos, *Dionysiaca Volume 1*, page 229.

The above passage describes the reason behind the Titanomachy. After it was over, Zeus reincarnated Zagreus.

> Semele was kept for a more brilliant union, for already Zeus ruling on high intended to make a new Dionysos grow up, a bullshaped copy of the older Dionysos; since he thought with regret of the illfated Zagreus. This was a son born to Zeus in dragonbed by Persephoeia, the consort of the blackrobed king of the underworld; when Zeus put on a deceiving shape of many coils, as a gentle dragon twining around her in lovely curves, and ravished the maidenhood of unwedded Persephoeia; though she was hidden when all that dwelt in Olympos were bewitched by this one girl, rivals in love for the marriageable maid and offered their dower for an unsmirched bridal.[13]

- Nonnos, *Dionysiaca Volume 1*, pages 207-209.

This was written about his father, Zeus.

> Belos on the Euphrates, called Ammon in Libya, thou art Apis by the Nile, Arabian Cronos, Assyrian Zeus! On thy fragrant altar, that thousand-year-old wise bird the phoenix lays sweet smelling woods with his curved claw, bringing the end of one life and the beginning of another; for there he is born again, self-begotten, the image of equal time renewed-he sheds old age in the fire, and from the fire takes in exchange youthful bloom. Be thou called Sarapis, the cloudless Zeus of Egypt; be thou Cronos, or Phethon of many names, or Mithras the Sun of Babylon, in Hellas

---

[12] Nonnos, *Dionysiaca Volume 1*, page 229.
[13] Nonnos, *Dionysiaca Volume 1*, pages 207-209.

Delphic Apollo; be thou Gamos, whom Love begat in shadowy dreams, fulfilling the deceptive desire of a mock union, when from sleeping Zeus, after he had sprinkled the damp seed over the earth with the self-wedding point of the sword, the heights brought forth by reason of the heavenly drops; be though painquelling Paieon or patterned Heaven; be though called the Starclad since by night starry mantles illuminate the sky- O hear my voice graciously with friendly ears! Such was the hymn of Dionysus.[14]

Plutarch wrote about Osiris and Isis, too. Plutarch was a Greek scholar who lived from 45 AD to 120 AD. He went to Rome and became a teacher. He wrote about many subjects and some of his famous works include the Moralia or Moral Essays. In one of these essays entitled Isis and Osiris, he wrote:

One of the first acts related of Osiris in his reign was to deliver the Egyptians from their destitute and brutish manner of living. This he did by showing them the fruits of cultivation, by giving them laws, and by teaching them to honour the gods. Later he travelled over the whole earth civilizing it without the slightest need of arms, but most of the peoples he won over to his way by the charm of this persuasive discourse combined with song and all manner of music. Hence the Greeks came to identify whim with Dionysus.

During his absence the tradition is that Typhon attempted nothing revolutionary because Isis, who was in control, was vigilant and alert; but when he returned home Typhon contrived a treacherous plot against him and formed a group of conspirators seventy-two in number. He had also the co-operation of a queen from Ethiopia who was there at the time and whose name they report as Aso. Typhon, having secretly measured Osiris's body and having made ready a beautiful chest of corresponding size artistically ornamented, caused it to be brought into the room where the festivity was in progress. The company was much pleased at the sight of it and admired it greatly, whereupon Typhon

---

[14] Nonnos, *Dionysiaca III*, Page 183.

jestingly promised to present it to the man who should find the chest to be exactly his length when he lay down in it. They all tried it in turn, but no one fitted it; then Osiris got into it and lay down, and those who were in the plot ran to it and slammed down the lid, which they fastened by nails from the outside and also by using molten lead. Then they carried the chest to the river and sent it on its way to the sea through the Tanitic Mouth. Wherefore the Egyptians even to this day name this mouth the hateful and execrable. Such is the tradition.[15]

After Isis retrieved the body of Osiris, she gave it a proper burial, but Typhon found it at night by the light of the moon and dismembered it into 14 parts. Isis was able to recover the parts except for the phallus.

The traditional result of Osiris's dismemberment is that there are many so-called tombs of Osiris in Egypt; for Isis held a funeral for each part when she had found it.[16]

Typhon-Set had red hair and a red complexion. The devil is depicted as a red-skinned, beastly man. As I will show, Set is Satan, the devil, Loki, Prometheus, Trickster, and other names yet to be found. The ancient Egyptians in favor of Osiris did rituals to insult Set including attacking red-haired men, or sacrificing red heifers. The Devil tarot card shows the devil with his torch of fire as Prometheus gave man fire. The woman is shown with grapes as the female was often associated with agriculture.

---

[15] Plutarch, *Moralia Volume V*, Page 37.
[16] Plutarch, *Moralia Volume V*, page 45.

http://en.wikipedia.org/wiki/File:RWS_Tarot_15_Devil.jpg (public domain)

The head is that of a goat, but the legs appear to be the legs of a beast. This is in reference to the combining of the Set lineage with the Pharaohs of Egypt. The pentagram that represents the five elements and the Cronide gods/goddesses associated with them (often Spirit is Zeus, Earth is Demeter, Fire is Hephaestus, Air is Athena, Water is Poseidon) is inverted as anything associated with Set is usually an inversion of symbols or ways established by Osiris,

Zeus, and all of the gods and goddesses of the Cronide line. The Set monster appears to be possibly an aardvark or jackal, but perhaps it may represent a coyote as well. The hippopotamus and pig were also associated with Set. The hand gesture is different and it appears to be similar to the Kohanite hand blessing. This devil symbol or depiction similar to the Baphomet. The devil is Set in this case but it can also refer to Cronus. Set was said to be bisexual as he attempted to rape Horus and Isis.

Now Osiris and Isis changed from good minor deities into gods. But the power of Typhon, weakened and crushed, but still fighting and struggling against extinction, they try to console and mollify by certain sacrifices; but again there are times when, at certain festivals, they humiliate and insult him by assailing red-headed men with jeering and by throwing an ass over the edge of a precipice, as the people of Kopto do, because Typhon had red hair and in colour resembled an ass. [17]

The Egyptians because of their belief tht Typhon was of red complexion, also dedicate to sacrifice such of their neat cattle as are of a red colour, but they conduct the examination of thee so scrupulously that, if an animal has but one hair black or white, they think it wrong to sacrifice it for they regard as suitable for sacrifice not what is dear to the gods but the reverse, namely, such animals as have incarnate in them souls of unholy and unrighteous men who have been transformed into other bodies. For this reason they involke curses on the head of the victim and cut it off, and in earlier times they used to throw it in the river, but now they sell it to aliens.[18]

Then again they depict Osiris by means of an eye and a scepter, the one of which indicates forethought and the other power, much as Homer in calling the Lord and King of all "Zeus supreme and counselor" appears by "supreme" to signify his prowess and by "counselor" his careful planning and thoughtfulness.[19]

---

[17] Plutarch, *Moralia Volume V*, page 73.
[18] Plutarch, *Moralia Volume V*, pages 75 - 77.
[19] Plutarch, *Moralia Volume V*, Pages 123-125.

Manetho was an Egyptian scholar who lived during the 3rd century BC. Manetho listed out the order of the gods, kings, and pharaohs and so did the Turin Papyrus:

The timing of this whole sequence of pantheons may be determined from the Egyptian Manetho King's List and the Egyptian Turin Papyrus. The Sumerian King's List appears to be correct in the king's name sequence, but the timing of ruler ship is in the hundreds of thousands of years whereas the Egyptian list is in the thousands of years for all of the kings.

As discussed in previous books, per my calculations and assumptions, a total of about 16,000 solar years ago, the first god ruled. The last pharaoh of Egypt was Caesarian. He was born on June 23, 47 BC (around the summer solstice) and was allegedly murdered on August 23, 30 BC. He reigned with his mother, jointly from September 2, 44 BC to his alleged death. Caesarian lived in Rome for two years of his life and returned back to Egypt with his mother after Caesar was assassinated on March 15, 44 BC (The Ides of March). There are some claims that Caesarian escaped to India and was not killed. Octavian took over the rulership of Egypt and Rome in 30 BC.

The Julian calendar and Gregorian calendar that we use today are based on the beginning of his reign. It was designed for him under commission of his father, Julius Caesar and his rulership began on September 02nd. Julius Caesar reformed the Roman calendar in 46 BC and it had a regular year of 365 days divided into 12 months. A leap day was added in February every four years. The Gregorian calendar was added to compensate with differences between it and a tropical solar year. It is also interesting to note that January 01 was not always the start of the New Year, it was around September 01. The Coptic Calendar, also called the Alexandrian Calendar, has its new year on September 11 and the calendar is based on the old Egyptian calendar. It is still used by the Coptic Church, today.

It appears there is about a 44 year difference between today's calendar start date (from year 01 BC to 01 AD) and the start of Caesarian's rule. However, this could be a mistake done on purpose to hide the true identity of the last pharaoh, Caesarian.

In conclusion, the secret of all of the old pantheons and forbidden books is expressed in the Mythological Unification Model by noting that the female and male archetypes are used to express natural cycles and embedded/encoded knowledge of science, medicine, astronomy, engineering, and more. These gods were real and the last main god was Dionysus who took on female characteristics and expressed himself through both female and male attributes. The mythological models were based on real people and real events and a combination of them. The writings of Plutarch, Nonnos, Manetho, and Diordorus Siculus include the story of Osiris-Dionysus going around the world after he civilized Egypt, teaching the people the arts of farming and animal husbandry and civilization before he was killed.

The Story of Earth maker giving Hare holy rites (medicine lodge used on certain days) to give to the people, from the Ho-Chunk stories, talks about Hare receiving rites from a higher god to benefit the people. This is similar to the story of Osiris-Dionysus and/or Zeus going around the world teaching humans the arts of civilization. There are stories on both sides of the globe of a being who taught rites/mysteries to benefit the people. There are other stories as well including the Mesoamerican stories of Quetzalcoatl and other similar gods giving their ancestors the knowledge of civilization and sacred rites.

Further study into ancient texts and oral traditions of mythology and ritual can be done, but in the end there will be some conflicting details because the stories have been slightly modified from culture to culture. However, the mythologies all consist of a core system/model which contains the creator gods, a civilizing god, the war of the gods, earth catastrophes amounting to extermination of previous races, the alleged creation of humans, the inter-breeding of humans with these gods/goddesses, a death of a god/goddess with their rebirth, and embedded knowledge of solar system, star, and earth cycles. The idea that these systems/models were given to the people in the past by a person/group of people to help them create civilizations after a major war/genocide, is the Mythological Unification Theory and is backed up by mythology, folklore, ancient artifacts, and ancient writings across the globe. The question of who the "ancient people" were before the current "human" is the next question that needs to be answered. It appears from the Greek writers that these ancient gods and goddesses were of large stature and had considerable strength. Dionysus was said to have brought back lions to his grandmother Rhea for her chariot at the age of nine.

Plato talked about Atlantis in Timeus and Critis. Hesiod talked about a great war between Zeus and the Titans, and Ovid wrote about the time periods of the human race in Metamorphosis. There was an elder race of giants.

It is said that Thera or Santorini is the ancient location of Atlantis. I believe this island was the home of Poseidon, Zeus' brother, as it is very close to Crete and Greece and Italy. I also believe there was a large land mass in the middle of the Atlantic Ocean that sank years before Zeus was even born.

Now let's take a look at some of the symbols of the ancient god Zeus and his son, Dionysus-Osiris. I believe the hand of Sabazios is probably inherited by Dionysus-Osiris from his father, Zeus.

Bronze hand used in the worship of Sabazios (British Museum). Roman 1st-2nd century CE.
http://en.wikipedia.org/wiki/File:HandOfSabazius.JPG
- public domain

The above picture is called the Hand of Sabazios. It has the symbols of the ram, the penis/pinecone, the wine, the fleur de lis, the altar, the serpent, and the two finger blessing and more.

The sacred animals of this god were the lion or any large cat, the serpent, the phoenix, the ram or any ram like animal such as the ibex, the ram, and the bull.

The pinecone topped thyrsus, the djed, and the staff were his weapon of conquest and his signature symbol of rulership.

He had priests and priestesses known as the bacchants, bacchantes, maenads, and satyrs.

He was the god of the orphans since he was orphaned and raised by his grandmother and at the mercy of his angry step-mother Hera. His mother Semele died apparently after childbirth.

He was a dual natured god. He preferred peace but would give war and death to those that deserved it. He was masculine and feminine. He loved purple robes and ivy wreaths and the drink of wine and beer. He could be ecstatic and frenzied or focused and controlled. He was cunning and could play the role of trickster and he could be truthful and sincere. He was the baphomet.

He took pity on the helpless and downtrodden. He made mistakes. In the end he was remembered and forgotten at the same time.

His gifts were those of civilization, agriculture, wine and beer making, love, and ecstasy. His campaign was to end the savagery of cannibalism and butchery of humans. The crook was used for shepherding and the flail was used for grains. The X or hooked X represents the crook and flail. So does the letter M. An upside down M is W and it represents Set, his supposed destroyer which represented the end of the planting and harvesting season.

His mysteries are everywhere. His mysteries include those of the great mother goddess because she taught him everything she knew which included agriculture, earth cycles, medicine, and sex mysteries. He honored her by wearing the woman's girdle and the purple robe. Some of his mysteries even included the knowledge of the titans that came before him and his grandmother's race. Before them, came a race of self-born beings of which will be examined in later writings. Perhaps they passed on their knowledge to the titans who passed it on to the Olympians who passed it on to the humans.

He taught the priests how to track the cycles of the planet by watching the sun patterns and stars. This is the basis of the temple, pyramid, mound, stonehenge or woodhenge. His mysteries were corrupted when priestesses were eliminated, human sacrifice and cannibalism crept back into the rites, and pedophilia became rampant amongst so called holy men.

His family is still with us, just not in physical form, watching and waiting for us to find them and restore them and the great mother's rites that can be summed up as eat, drink, and be merry; harm ye none; and take care of the orphans and widows.

According to Wikipedia, Plutarch believed the Jewish God was Dionysus. Valerius Maximus believed it was Zeus. Sanchoniathon believed it was Cronus.

The first Jews who settled in Rome were expelled in 139 BCE, along with Chaldaean astrologers by Cornelius Hispalus under a law which proscribed the propagation of the "corrupting" cult of "Jupiter Sabazius," according to the epitome of a lost book of Valerius Maximus:

Gnaeus Cornelius Hispalus, praetor peregrinus in the year of the consulate of Marcus Popilius Laenas and Lucius Calpurnius, ordered the astrologers by an edict to leave Rome and Italy within ten days, since by a fallacious interpretation of the stars they perturbed fickle and silly minds, thereby making profit out of their lies. The same praetor compelled the Jews, who attempted to infect the Roman custom with the cult of Jupiter Sabazius, to return to their homes."
By this it is conjectured that the Romans identified the Jewish Yahweh Saboas ("of the Hosts") as Jove Sabazius.

This mistaken connection of Sabazios and Sabaos has often been repeated. In a similar vein, Plutarch maintained that the Jews worshipped Dionysus, and that the day of Sabbath was a festival of Sabazius. Plutarch also discusses the identification of the Jewish god with the "Egyptian" (actually archaic Greek) Typhon, an identification which he later rejects, however (though the identification of Typhon-Seth and YHWH is not really controversial, as it is well attested to in Hebrew practice from the 4th century BC through the 1st century AD). The monotheistic Hypsistarians worshipped the Jewish god under this name.

I don't believe this is a mistake. In fact, the Nag Hammadi Library confirms this and states that the god of the Jews was called the Demiurge, Saklas, Samael, and Sabaoth who was taken up to the 7th heaven by the great goddess Barbelos and taught her mysteries. This is the same thing as Rhea teaching the mysteries to Dionysus or Gaia and Delphinic Apollo combining mysteries at the Oracle of Delphi with Dionysus. Delphinic Apollo appears to be Zeus. Again, there are variations in the names and slight changes in the story. But the story is the same once you begin to compare mythologies from around the world. This is the great secret that is kept from the masses. The identity of the gods and goddesses and their mysteries are coming back and will be in full presentation to the people and no so called "holy" man can stop this.

Chapter 3

The Olympians and Ariadne-Isis

The Olympians were ancient Greek gods and goddesses that were related to Zeus who sat on Mt. Olympus and decided the fate of humans and gods. The Olympians included Zeus, Hera, Poseidon, Demeter, Athena, Hestia, Apollo, Artemis, Ares, Aphrodite, Hephaestus, and Hermes. Hestia was often replaced by Dionysus. Sometimes, Hades and Persephone were included with the Olympians as well as Heracles and Aesclypius.

Valerius Maximus identified the Abrahamic God as Jupiter Sabazius, which is another name for Zeus. Dionysus-Osiris was his son and the reincarnation of Zagreus. Ariadne was the wife of Dionysus-Osiris. She was daughter of King Minos, another son of Zeus by Europa.

The Roman equivalent of the Greek Gods just changed some of the names of the gods and goddesses and equated them with the planets in our solar system or other names.

Zeus is the Roman Jupiter

Hera is the Roman Juno

Hades is Pluto

Poseidon is Neptune

Demeter is Ceres (which is named after some large asteroid in the asteroid belt betweeen Mars and Jupiter)

Hestia is Vesta

Aphrodite is Venus

Ares is Mars

Hepheastus is Vulcan (an alleged planet in our solar system, that can't be seen from the Earth)

Hermes is Mercury

Apollo is the Sun or sometimes Phoebus

Artemis is Diana or the moon

Athena is Minerva

Dionysus is Bacchus or Sabazios

Heracles is Hercules

Persephone is Proserpina

The rest of the Greek gods and goddesses were also adopted by the Romans and given Roman names. Their stories were adopted and written about by Roman/Latin writers as well.

The Olympians gained their power after a war between Zeus and the Titans. After that, Zeus reigned supreme and passed down rulership to his bloodline, only. Those that opposed his laws, were destroyed. Hesiod and Homer wrote about the Olympians. Hesiod's work called *Theogony and Work of Days* includes the story of the Titanomachy. His writing includes over 800 verses in poetic form describing five ages of man, advice, the war, and more. Here is what he wrote.

> **For a long time they fought in bitter toil**
> **Against one another in strong battles,**
> **The Titan gods and those born of Cronus,**
> **The proud Titans from lofty Orthrys**
> **And from Olympus the gods, givers of good,**
> **whom fair-haired Rhea bore, having lain with Cronus.**
> **With bitter war against one another**
> **They fought continually for ten full years;**
> **There was no end or relief from harsh strife**
> **for either, the war's outcome was evenly balanced.**
> **But when he gave them everything fitting,**
> **nectar and ambrosia, which the gods eat themselves,**
> **and the proud spirit grew in the breasts of all,**
> **[when they tasted nectar and lovely ambrosia]**
> **then the father of gods and men said to them:**
> **"Hear me, good children of Earth and Sky,**

> that I may say what the spirit in my chest commands.
> For a long time now against one another
> we have fought every day for victory and power,
> the Titan gods and we born of Cronus.
> Show your great force and unbeatable arms
> against the titans in savage war;
> remember our friendship, and how much you suffered
> before you came to the light from grievous bondage
> inder the murky gloom, thanks to our counsels."

Hesiod continues with the war not ending and the male and female titans still wanting to fight:

> A hundred arms shot from the shoulders
> of each and all, fifty heads grew from the
> shoulders of each, from their massive bodies.
> They stood against the Titans in grim battle,
> holding great rocks in their massive hands;
> the Titans opposite brought force to their ranks
> expectantly; both displayed the deeds of arms
> and strength together, and the vast sea echoed loudly
> and the earth resounded greatly, and the wide sky
> shook and groaned, and great Olympus was shaken
> from its foundation by the immortals' charge; a heavy
> tremor of feet reached dim Tartarus, and the loud
> noise of unspeakable rout and strong weapons;
> so they hurled at each other painful weapons;
> shouts from both sides reached starry Sky,
> As they came together with a great outcry,
>
> Zeus no longer restrained his might, but now his

> heart was filled with wrath, and he revealed all
> his force; from the sky and Olympus both,
> he came throwing a lightning-flurry; the bolts
> flew thick with thunder and lightning
> from his massive hand, whirling a holy flame,
> one after another; the life-giving earth resounded
> in flames, the vast woods crackled loudly about,
> all the land and Ocean's streams and the
> barren sea were boiling; the hot blast enveloped
> the land-born Titans, the flame reached the upper
> brightness in its furry; although they were strong, the blazing
> glow of thunder and lightning blinded their eyes.
> The awful heat seized Chasm; it seemed,
> for eyes to see and ears to hear the sound,
> just as if earth and wide sky from above came
> together; for so great a noise would arise
> from the one fallen upon and the other falling down';
> such a noise arose from the strife of clashing gods.
> the winds stirred up earthquake and dust and
> thunder and lighting and blazing lightning-bolt,
> the weapons of great Zeus, and brought the shout
> And cry into the midst of both sides; a great din
> arose from fearful strife and strength's work was revealed.[20]

Now what kind of a weapon would burn the water and the earth in such a manner? It sounds like a nuclear bomb or a laser weapon. The attack from Zeus came from the sky, too. This poem appears to be a description of a highly advanced warfare that lasted ten years and was fought from the air.

---

[20] Hesiod, *Theogony and Work of Days*, Page 48.

There are numerous stories around the world about a great war. So here, the thunderbolt weapon of Zeus, was advanced enough to be used from the sky to burn the earth and the waters. This sounds like a directed energy weapon, perhaps in combination with nuclear bombs.

So after this war, Zeus sent his son, Dionysus-Osiris out to civilize the world and end cannibalism. We know from Egyptian mythology that Isis was the wife of Osiris. She was Ariadne, the daughter of King Minos and his wife, and his queen Pasiphaë, daughter of Helios, the Sun-Titan. She is famous for her part in the story of the Minotaur from Crete.

She helped Theseus kill the Minotaur and find his way out of the labyrinth on Crete. She was in charge of the labyrinth where Athenian sacrifices were made as reparations for killing King Minos' son. Theseus agreed to marry her, but abandoned her on an island called Naxos. It is here, that Dionysus finds her and marries her.

In the writings of Nonnos, a tale of Theseus abandoning Ariadne and Dionysus-Osiris finding her crying after it, is given. He marries her and loves her dearly and she becomes his queen and mother of his children. There is one tale of Dionysus having an affair with another maiden during his travels but even though she was distraught over it, Ariadne forgives him. She had several children with Dionysus, including Oenopion, the personification of wine, Staphylus (related to grapes), Thoas, Peparethus, Phanus, Eurymedon, Enyeus, Ceramus, Maron, Euanthes, Latramys and Tauropolis. The Vatican has a statue of a sleeping Ariadne inside the Vatican museum.

Ariadne is the Cretan goddess holding snakes in her hand while being bare-breasted. Ariadne is Isis. Here is some of her story from The Dionysiaca by Nonnos.

> **Dionysos, why do you still bear a grudge against the cestus that makes marriage? Beroe was no proper bride for Bacchos, but this marriage of the sea was quite fitting, because I joined the daughter of Aphrodite of the sea to a husband whose path is in the sea. I have kept a daintier one for your bridechamber, Ariadne, of the family of Minos, and your kin. Leave Amymone to the sea, a nobody, one of the family of the sea herself. You must leave the mountains of Lebanon and the waters of Adonis and go to Phrygia, the land of lovely girls; there awaits you a bride without salt water, Aura of Titan stock. Thrace the friend of brides will receive you, with a wreath of victory ready and a bride's bower; thither Pallene also the**

shakespear summons you, beside whose chamber I will crown you with a wedding wreath for your prowess, when you have own Aphrodite's delectable wrestling-match,

So wild Eros spoke to his love mad brother Bacchos: then he flapt his whizzing fiery wings, and the sham bird flew in the skies travelling until he came to the house of Zeus. And from the Assyrian gulf Dionysos went daintily clad into the Lydian land along the plain of Pactolos where the dark water is reddened by the gold gleaming mud of wealthy lime; he entered Maionia, and stood before Rheia his mother, offering royal gifts from the Indian sea. Then leaving the stream of the river of deep riches, and the Phyrygian plain, and the nation of soft living men, he planted his vine on the northerly plain, and passed from the towns of Asia to the cities of Europe.[21]

Minos was the son of Zeus and Europa and was the king of Crete. Ariadne was his daughter as I said before. So here you see the in-breeding taking place. Aura was a maiden that Dionysus fell in love with, but she did not want him. Amymone was the daughter of Aphrodite and was married to Poseidon.

---

[21] Nonnos, *Dionysiaca Volume 3*, pages 297.

Chapter 4

The Stories of the Greek Gods and Goddesses

Per my research, I believe the Zeus bloodline existed about 12,000 to 25,000 years ago. This bloodline travelled the world and taught the mysteries of science, agriculture, biology, medicine, math, astronomy, and many other things including laws to live by. This great bloodline interbred with one another while all other bloodlines of the titans were mostly exterminated. Everyone has a story to tell and the winners of this war between this Cronide bloodline and the Titans, is quite a tale.

Zeus was considered the father of the Gods and humans. He had many mates much to the chagrin of his wife, Hera who hated all of his illegitimate children. He was raised by Rhea on Mount Ida among sheeps and goats. He hid in a cave from his father. When he was grown, he battled the Titans and became the supreme ruler. He had his children (both sons and daughters) travel the world after this war and after the planet had sunken into cannibalism and savagery, to civilize it. His symbols include the thunderbolt, the eagle or phoenix, the snake, the goat and ram, the bull, bull horns, and the throne.

Hera was the wife of Zeus. She bore him two sons: Hephaestus and Ares and four daughters: Hebe, Enyo, Eileithyia, and Eris. She hated all of Zeus' bastard children and consorts and plotted against them. It is said she took part in the plot to kill Zagreus. She was hung up in the sky by Zeus because of this, until her son, Hephaestus rescued her. She is Queen of the gods. Her symbols include a lotus scepter, a peacock, and a crown. She assisted Jason and the Argonauts and the Greeks during the Trojan War. She is also goddess of marriage.

Hades was the god of the underworld or the dead. He is shown with a two-pronged staff and a 3-headed dog, named Cerebus. He is said to have captured Persephone and raped her. He is said to be brother to Zeus and Poseidon, but in some texts he is equated with Zeus.

Poseidon is the god of the sea and the brother of Zeus. He married the daughter of Aphrodite. His symbols are the 3-pronged scepter, the dolphin, and the shell. He has many children by consorts as well.

Hestia was the sister of Zeus. She is said to have discovered the art of making a home. She is goddess of the home and hearth. She remained unmarried.

Demeter is the goddess of the harvest. She is the sister of Zeus and is associated with the cornucopia and Eleusinian mysteries. She is said to have discovered many agricultural fruits. She had a daughter named Persephone/Kore with Zeus.

Apollo was the son of Zeus by Leto. He was the twin brother of Artemis and was the god of the sun, music, and medicine. He had many children with consorts, but was in love with his sister, Artemis who refused to marry him. His symbols include the laurel wreath, the lyre, the medicine bag, and the sun.

Ares was the war god and son of Zeus and Hera. He was ruthless. His sons Romulus and Remus are said to have started the city of Rome and the Amazons were his daughters.

Hermes was the son of Zeus through Maia. He is the god of writing, language, medicine, and math. His symbols include the caduceus, the winged helmet, and the winged boots.

Athena is the daughter of Zeus. Some say she was born only by him out of his head, others say she was from Zeus and Metis. She was the goddess of war, crafts, magic, and science. She was never married. Her symbols include the helmet, spear, and shield. She is said to have had a son with Hephaestus.

Artemis was the sister of Apollo and daughter of Zeus and Leto. She was the goddess of the hunt. Her sacred animals were the bear and the dear. She fell in love with a hunter named Orion, who was killed by a wild boar. Her symbol is the bow.

Persephone was a daughter of Zeus and Demeter. She was abducted and raped and taken away from her mother by Hades or Zeus.

Dionysus was the god of wine and civilization. He was the son of Zeus and Semele and said to be the reincarnation of Zagreus. His symbols include the grapes and wine cup. His sacred animals were the lion, the goat, the bull, and the snake. He also wore a feathered cap.

Heracles was the son of Zeus and Alcmene. He was known for his physical strength.

Hephaestus was married to Aphrodite. He was the son of Zeus and Hera. He was the smith of the gods.

Aphrodite was the daughter of Zeus and Dione. She had many lovers and many children. She is the goddess of love and her symbol is the dove and seashell.

Gaia was the mother of all gods and titans. She created her consort and created all of the giants and other beings.

Ouranus was the consort of Gaia. He was castrated by his son, Cronus, who took over the throne.

Cronus was a titan who married his sister Rhea. Together they bore the Cronides. He swallowed his children because a prophecy stated one of them would overthrow him. His symbols include the sickle and the planet Saturn. Saturn is symbolic of the Cronide bloodline. The Star of David/Seal of Solomon/Hexagram is the symbol that represents Saturn or the Cronide bloodline.

Rhea was the mother of Zeus, Poseidon, Hades, Demeter, Hestia, and Hera. Her symbols include the drum, bees, turrette crown, and lions.

The original twelve titans created from Gaia were the following:

Oceanus and Tethys,
Hyperion and Theia,
Coeus and Phoebe,
Cronus and Rhea,
Mnemosyne, Themis,
Crius, Iapetus

Children of Oceanus:
Oceanids, Potamoi, Calypso

Children of Hyperion:
Helios, Selene, Eos

Daughters of Coeus:
Leto and Asteria

Sons of Iapetus:

Atlas, Prometheus, Epimetheus, Menoetius

Sons of Crius:

Astraeus, Pallas, Perses

The Titans are also credited with many scientific discoveries in the ancient writings of Diordorus Siculus.

All of these ancient titans and Olympians taught knowledge. Their teachings are part of the mystery schools. The Mithrac cult, Orphic cult, and Abrahamic Religion cults are all from the ancient Zeus cults. I will delve into the mysteries of the Orphic cult in a later writings as it it is an interesting one that casts the ancient god as a hermaphrodite. This should ring a bell for those that are familiar with the Baphomet or the Gnostic Writings from the Nag Hammadi Library. The Eleusinian mysteries are associated with the goddess cults such as Rhea and Demeter. According to Wikipedia:

> **The Eleusinian Mysteries (Greek: Ἐλευσίνια Μυστήρια) were initiation ceremonies held every year for the cult of Demeter and Persephone based at Eleusis in ancient Greece. Of all the mysteries celebrated in ancient times, these were held to be the ones of greatest importance. It is acknowledged that their basis was an old agrarian cult which probably goes back to the Mycenea period (c. 1600 – 1100 BC) and it is believed that the cult of Demeter was established in 1500 BC. The idea of immortality which appears in syncretistic religions of antiquity was introduced in late antiquity. The mysteries represented the myth of the abduction of Persephone from her mother Demeter by the king of the underworld Hades, in a cycle with three phases, the "descent" (loss), the "search" and the "ascent", with the main theme the "ascent" of Persephone and the reunion with her mother. It was a major festival during the Hellenic era, and later spread to Rome. The name of the town, Eleusís seems to be Pre-Greek and it is probably a counterpart with Elysium and the goddess Eileithyia.**
>
> **The rites, ceremonies, and beliefs were kept secret and consistently preserved from a hoary antiquity. The initiated believed that they would have a reward in the**

afterlife. There are many paintings and pieces of pottery that depict various aspects of the Mysteries. Since the Mysteries involved visions and conjuring of an afterlife, some scholars believe that the power and longevity of the Eleusinian Mysteries came from psychedelic agents."

To participate in these mysteries one had to swear a vow of secrecy. Four categories of people participated in the Eleusinian Mysteries:

1. Priests, priestesses and hierophants.
2. Initiates, undergoing the ceremony for the first time.
3. Others who had already participated at least once. They were eligible for the fourth category.
4. Those who had attained *épopteia* (Greek: ἐποπτεία) (English: "contemplation"), who had learned the secrets of the greatest mysteries of Demeter.

There were two Eleusinian Mysteries, the Greater and the Lesser. According to Thomas Taylor, "the dramatic shows of the Lesser Mysteries occultly signified the miseries of the soul while in subjection to the body, so those of the Greater obscurely intimated, by mystic and splendid visions, the felicity of the soul both here and hereafter, when purified from the defilements of a material nature and constantly elevated to the realities of intellectual [spiritual] vision." And that according to Plato, "the ultimate design of the Mysteries … was to lead us back to the principles from which we descended, … a perfect enjoyment of intellectual [spiritual] good."

The Lesser Mysteries took place in the month of Anthesteria under the direction of Athens' *archon basileus*. In order to qualify for initiation, participants would sacrifice a piglet to Demeter and Persephone, and then ritually purify themselves in the river Illisos. Upon completion of the Lesser Mysteries, participants were deemed *mystai* ("initiates") worthy of witnessing the Greater Mysteries.[22]

---

[22] Wikipedia

Ovid was a Roman poet that lived from 43 BC to 17AD. He wrote an epic poem called *Metamorphoses*. According to Wikipedia:

The *Metamorphoses*, Ovid's most ambitious and popular work, consists of a 15-book catalogue written in dactylic hexameter about the transformations in Greek and Roman mythology set within a loose mytho-historical framework. Each myth is set outdoors where the mortals are often vulnerable to external influences. Almost 250 different myths are mentioned. The poem stands in the tradition of mythological and aetiological catalogue poetry such as Hesiod's *Catalogue of Women*, Callimachus' *Aetia*, Nicander's *Heteroeumena*, and Parthenius' *Metamorphoses*. The first book describes the formation of the world, the ages of man, the flood, the story of Daphne's rape by Apollo and Io's by Jupiter. The second book opens with Phaethon and continues describing the love of Jupiter with Callisto and Europa. The third book focuses on the mythology of Thebes with the stories of Cadmus, Actaeon, and Pentheus. The fourth book focuses on three pairs of lovers: Pyramus and Thisbe, Salmacis and Hermaphroditus, and Perseus and Androma. The fifth book focuses on the song of the Muses, which describes the rape of Proserpina. The sixth book is a collection of stories about the rivalry between gods and mortals, beginning with Arachne and ending with Philomela. The seventh book focuses on Medea, as well as Cephalus and Procris. The eighth book focuses on Daedalus' flight, the Calydonian boar hunt, and the contrast between pious Baucis and Philemon and the wicked Erysichthon. The ninth book focuses on Heracles and the incestuous Byblis. The tenth book focuses on stories of doomed love, such as Orpheus, who sings about Hyacinthus, as well as Pygmalion, Myrrha, and Adonis. The eleventh book compares the marriage of Peleus and Thetis with the love of Ceyx and Alcyone. The twelfth book moves from myth to history describing the exploits of Achilles, the battle of the centaurs, and Iphigeneia. The thirteenth book discusses the contest over Achilles' arms, and Polyphemus. The fourteenth moves to Italy, describing the journey of Aeneas, Pomona and Vertumnus, and Romulus. The final book opens with a philosophical lecture by Pythagoras and the deification of Caesar.

The end of the poem praises Augustus and expresses Ovid's belief that his poem has earned him immortality.

Here is some of his poem regarding the giants of old:

The Metamorphoses of Ovid Translated by Allen Mandelbaum

Book 1

My soul would sing of metamorphoses. But since o gods, you were the source of these bodies becoming other bodies, breathe your breath into my book of changes: may the song I sing be seamless as its way weaves from the world's beginning to our day.

Before the sea and lands began to be, before the sky had mantled everything, then all of nature's face was featureless- what men call chaos; undigested mass of crude, confused, and scumbled elements, a heap of seeds that clashed, of things mismatched. There was no Titan Sun to light the world, no crescent Moon-no Phoebe-to renew her slender horns; in the surrounding air, earth's weight had yet to find its balanced state; and Amphitrite's arms had not yet stretched along the farthest margins of the land. For though the sea and land and air were there, the land could not be walked upon, the sea could not be sum, the air was without splendor nothing maintained its shape; all were at war; in some same body cold and hot would battle; the damp contended with the dry, things hard with soft, and weighty things with weightless parts.

A god-and nature, now become benign-ended this strife. He separated sky and earth, and earth and waves, and he defined pure air and thicker air. Unraveling these things from their blind heap, assigning each its place-distinct-he linked them all in peace. Fire, the weightless force of heaven's dome, shot up; it occupied the highest zone. Just under fire, the light air found its home.

In book 2, Lucifer is mentioned:

And while-amazed-audacious Phaethon gazed at this splendid handiwork, alert aurora, as the east shone, opened wide her purple gates, her halls rich with rose light. The stars retreat; their ranks are driven off by Lucifer who is the last to leave his station in the sky.

When Phoebus saw that Lucifer was gone, that all the world was tinged with red, and that the moon's slim horns had faded he commanded the swift Hours to yoke his steeds.[23]

It is interesting to note, that Metamorphoses attempts to answer what the past was like before the gods and goddesses existed.

---

[23] Wikipedia

Chapter 5

Manetho Timeline, Red Horn, White Buffalo Woman, and Red-Haired Giants

It is my opinion that the ancient Greek gods and goddesses were real people and they existed around 12,000 to 25,000 years ago. The ancient texts describe the wars they had and the final winner being the god known as Zeus and his bloodline, the Cronids. I've talked about the inbreeding that was delibertly done with this bloodline. I've talked about the Titans and their loss. I've revealed the Abrahamic God as Jupiter Sabazius, another name for Zeus. I've quoted some of the works from Greek and Roman scholars. I've shown you the texts that tell how Dionysus-Osiris travelled the world with his family and an army and civilized it. Now it's time to look at some of the other mythologies from around the world. The timeline of this whole sequence of pantheons may be determined from the Egyptian Manetho King's List and the Egyptian Turin Papyrus.

Manetho was an Egyptian priest from Heliopolis who lived in Egypt during Ptolemaic times. He tried to record the history of Egypt. He wrote *Aegyptiaca* (*History of Egypt*). In it he listed the reign of the gods on down to the pharaohs.

The Sumerian King's List appears to be correct in the kings' name sequence, but the timing of rulership is in the hundreds of thousands of years whereas the Egyptian list is in the thousands of years for all of the kings.

The Turin King List is also known as the Turin Royal Canon that lists the reigns of gods of old and kings from ancient Egypt. The chronology of the pharaohs of Egypt is listed for the dynasties before Ramses II. The list, lists the names of rulers and their length of reigns in years, months and days. The timing of these reigns corresponds to the Manetho list. The papyrus was found by the Italian traveler Bernardino Drovetti in 1820 at Luxor and is now sitting in the

Egyptian Museum in Turin, Italy. Manetho even mentions a white female pharaoh who built one of the pyramids.

Column 1 — Gods of Ancient Egypt beginning with Ptah and the Great Ennead

Turin King List	Manetho (Egyptian equivalent)
Ptah	Hephaestus (Ptah)
Ra	Helios (Ra)
-	Sosis or Agathosdaimon (perhaps Sothis?) (Shu)
Geb	Kronos (Geb)
Osiris	Osiris
Set	Typhon (Set)
Horus	Horus
Thoth	Thoth
Ma'at	Ma'at

Column 2 — Rows 1-10 Spirits and mythical kings

Column 2 — Rows 11-25 (Dynasties 1-2)

Column 3 — Rows 1-25 (Dynasties 2-5)

Column 4 — Rows 1-26 (Dynasties 6-8/9/10)

Column 5 — Rows 12-25 (Dynasties 11-12)

Column 6 — Rows 1-2 (Dynasties 12-13)

Column 7 — Rows 1-23 (Dynasty 13)

Column 8 — Rows 1-27 (Dynasty 13-14)

Column 9 — Rows 1-30 (Dynasty 14)

Column 10 — Rows 1-30 (Dynasties 14-15)

Column 11 — Rows 1-17 (Dynasties 16-17) [24]

According to Manetho the kingship period was as follows:

Rulership	Years
First Man /(God) was Hephaestus (Ptah)	727 ¾ solar years
Helios	80 1/8 solar year
Sosis	56 7/12 years
Cronos	40 ½ solar years
Osiris	35 solar years
Typhon	29 solar years
Orus	25 solar years
Bydus	Passed down to him after gods and demigods 13,900 lunar years (Egyptian year could equal a month of today) or 1255 solar years
Line of Kings	1817 solar years
Kings of Memphis	1790 solar years
Kings of this	350 solar years

---

[24] Wikipedia, Turin King List.

Rule of Spirits of the Dead and Demigods	5813 solar years
Pharoahs	3200 solar years
Caesarian till now	2000 solar years from last pharaoh

[25]

Over 16,000 solar years ago, the first god ruled. It is possible the years are not solar and it is also possible there were some mistakes in interpretation. With surety, the last 5100 years have recorded inscriptions and evidence backing up the timing. The Sumerian King's List goes back hundreds of thousands of years ago and some psychics like Edgar Cayce claim the first war occurred in Atlantis about 50,000 years ago. It is hard to say what is the most accurate, but I would probably believe the Egyptian source, more.

The last pharaoh of Egypt was Caesarion. He was born on June 23, 47 BC (around the summer solstice) and was allegedly murdered on August 23, 30 BC. He reigned with his mother, jointly from September 2, 44 BC to his alleged death. Caesarion lived in Rome for two years of his life and returned back to Egypt with his mother after Caesar was assassinated on March 15, 44 BC (The Ides of March). There are some claims that Caesarion escaped to India and was not killed. Octavian took over the rulership of Egypt and Rome in 30 BC.

The Julian calendar and Gregorian calendar that we use today are based on the beginning of his reign. It was designed for him under commission of his father, Julius Caesar and his rulership began on September 02nd. Julius Caesar reformed the Roman Calendar in 46 BC and it had a regular year of 365 days divided into 12 months. A leap day was added in February every four years. The Gregorian calendar was added to compensate with differences between it and a tropical solar year. It is also interesting to note that January 01 was not always the start of the new year, it was around September 01. The Coptic Calendar, also called the Alexandrian

---

[25] Manetho, *Aegypticaca translated by W.G. Waddell*, Pages 15-20.

Calendar, has its new year on September 11 and the calendar is based on the old Egyptian calendar. It is still used by the Coptic church, today.

The writings of Plutarch, Nonnos, and Diodorus Siculus include a story about Dionysus-Osiris going around the world after he civilized Egypt, teaching the people farming and animal husbandry and civilization before he was killed. The Story of Earthmaker giving Hare holy rites (medicine lodge used on certain days) to give to the people, from the Ho-Chunk stories, talks about Hare receiving rites from a higher god to benefit the people. This is similar to the story of Osiris and/or Zeus going around the world teaching humans the arts of civilization. So now there are stories on both sides of the globe of a being who taught rites/mysteries to benefit the people. There are other stories as well including the Mesoamerican stories of Queztlcoatl, Virococcha, Votan and other similar gods giving their ancestors the knowledge of civilization and sacred rites. According to Wikipedia:

> **Red Horn is a culture hero in Siouan oral traditions, specifically of the Ioway and Hocąk (Winnebago) nations. Only in Hocąk literature is he known as "Red Horn"** (*Hešucka*)**, but among the Ioway and Hocągara both, he is known by one of his variant names, "He Who Wears (Man) Faces on His Ears". This name derives from the living faces on his earlobes (Hocąk), or earbobs that come to life when he places them on his ears (Ioway). Elsewhere, he is given yet another name, "Red Man"** (*Wąkšucka*)**, on account of the fact that his entire body is red from head to toe. Red Horn was one of the five sons of Earthmaker whom the Creator fashioned with his own hands and sent to earth to rescue mankind. During his sojourn on earth, he contested both giants and water spirits, and led war parties against the bad spirits who plagued mankind. As Wears Faces on His Ears, he is also said to be a star, although its identity is a subject of controversy. Under the names "One Horn"** (*Hejąkiga*) **and "Without Horns"** (*Herok'aga*)**, he and his sons are chiefs over the lilliputian hunting spirits known as the** *herok'a* **and the "little children spirits". Red Horn, as chief of the** *herok'a***, has a spiritual and sometimes corporeal identity with the arrow. Archaeologists have speculated that Red Horn is a mythic figure in**

Mississippian art, represented on a number of Southeastern Ceremonial Complex (SECC) artifacts.

According to legend, Red Horn is one of the five great soteriological spirits fashioned by the Creator's own hands, sent to earth to make the world safe for the least endowed of Earthmaker's creation, the "two-legged walkers". The first spirit to be sent down to earth to help mankind was Trickster (*Wakdjąkaga*), whose foolishness made it necessary to recall him. Earthmaker next sent down Bladder (*Wadexuga*), whose arrogance led to the loss of all but one of his 20 brothers, so he too was recalled. Then Earthmaker made Turtle (*Kecągega*) and charged him to teach the humans how to live, but Turtle brought them war, and was in his turn recalled. The fifth and last of these heroes dispatched by Earthmaker was Hare (*Wacdjįgega*), who conquered all the bad spirits who had preyed on humanity. By accident, however, he introduced death, but made up for it by creating the Medicine Lodge, by whose discipline members could achieve immortality. Earthmaker made Hare in charge of this earth, and to each of the other three spirits he gave an otherworldly paradise to govern. The penultimate savior figure in this series was Redhorn. He had quite nearly succeeded, but was killed in a wrestling match with the enemies of the human race. Although later revived, he too was recalled, although the reasons for his failure are obscure. One source suggests that it was a lack of gravitas.

Then Earthmaker (*Mą'ųna*) sent down another son, He who Wears Human Heads as Earrings. He went around talking to people, but they would always fix on his earrings which were actual, living, miniature human heads. When these little heads saw someone looking at them, they would wink and make funny faces. In the end, He who Wears Human Heads as Earrings could not accomplish the mission either.

Hare sounds like Zeus, and Red Horn sounds like Dionysus-Osiris. Again, according to Wikipedia:

The adventures of Red Horn are set out in a set of stories known as the "Red Horn Cycle". The Red Horn Cycle depicts his adventures with Turtle, the thunderbird Storms-as-He-Walks (*Mą'e-manįga*) and others who contest a race of giants, the *Wąge-rucge* or "Man-Eaters", who have been killing human beings whom Red Horn has pledged to help. In the episode associated with this name, Red Horn turns himself into an arrow to win a race. After winning the race Red Horn creates heads on his earlobes and makes his hair into a long red braid called a *he*, "horn", in Hocąk. Thus he becomes known as "Red-horn" (*he-šucka*) and as "He who Wears (Human) Faces on His Ears" (*įco-horúšika*). In one episode an orphan girl who always wears a white beaverskin wrap is pressured by her grandmother to court Red Horn. Despite the girl's adamant refusal, the grandmother insists. She eventually relents and goes off to find Red Horn, who is surrounded by other girls. She teases him, and unexpectedly, he smiles at her. The other girls were jealous, they push and shove her and tell her "You don't know anything." Red Horn and his friends prepare to go on the warpath and are camped just outside the village. During this time the women bring the warriors moccasins and the she brings a pair to Red Horn, who accepts them. When the warriors return from battle, they play a prank and have the sentries proclaim that Red Horn and one of his friends are dead. The grandmother begins to cut the hair of the orphan girl, as if she were already Red Horn's wife. When he comes into view and it is apparent that he is not dead, the grandmother laments "I have wrecked my granddaughter's hair." The victors dance for four days, and many of the young men approach Red Horn to recommend their sisters to him. He takes no interest, and asks instead, "Where does the girl in the white beaverskin wrap live?" At night Red Horn shows up at the girl's lodge and lies down next to her. Her grandmother throws a blanket over them and they are married. In another episode, with their lives staked on the outcome, the giants challenge Red Horn and his friends to play *kisik* (lacrosse). The best giant player was a woman with long red hair just like Red Horn's. The little heads on Red Horn's ears caused her to laugh so much that it interfered with her game and the giants lost, but Red Horn married the girl with the red hair. The giants lost all the other contests as well. Then they challenged Red Horn and his friends to a wrestling match in which they threw all but Red Horn's friend Turtle. Since Red Horn and his fellow spirits lost two out of the three matches, they were all slain.

The two wives of Red Horn were pregnant at the time of his death. Red Horn's first wife, the girl in the white beaverskin wrap, gave birth to a son who had the same red hair and human heads hanging from his ears as his father. Red Horn's second wife, the giantess, also gave birth to a red haired boy, but with living faces where his nipples should have been. The sons were spared by the giants and grew up to be very large. One day the eldest son went out to fast in order to get a blessing from the thunderbirds. He went to seek his visions at a place not far from a broad prairie where the giants had a village. He knew that the head of his father, whose hair had by now turned white, hung from a lodge pole there. When he called out to the spirits with a death song, the kind sung by prisoners about to be executed, the giants who heard it would immediately jump into the fire. When the old men of the village saw that so many of their people were jumping in the flames, they guessed at the cause, and ordered four warriors to guard the scalp pole. Two of the guards painted themselves red and the others painted themselves black. Red Horn's two sons decided then to retrieve the heads of their father and his friends. They use their powers to make special red and black arrows to kill the guards, then grabbed the heads and ran with them. As the boys ran they shot the giants with their arrows, each arrow killing many giants. When they ran out of arrows, they used their bows as clubs, almost wiping out the giants completely. A little girl with a boy that she packed on her back are spared so that the race of giants do not become extinct, but they are thrown to the other side of the sea so than will no longer be a threat. The two sons then burn the bodies of the giants and grind up their bones and spread the powder around their own village. The two sons take the head of Red Horn and ask their mothers to sleep with it, but each replies, "How can I sleep with that, it is only a skull?" The boys take all three heads and lay them in a bed in the middle of the lodge. The next day Red Horn, Turtle, and Storms as He Walks are all found alive and sleeping in the bed. Where the sons had scattered the powdered bones of the

giants, all the people that the giants had killed were also found alive and sleeping. When Red Horn's wives saw this, they shouted, "Oh, our sons have brought our husbands back to life again!" The boys picked up their fathers and carried them around like children. In honor of this feat, Turtle and Storms as He Walks promise the boys special weapons. In another episode, the sons of Red Horn decide to go on the warpath. The older brother asks Storms as He Walks for the Thunderbird Warbundle. After some effort, it is produced, but the thunderbirds demand that it have a case. A friend of the sons of Red Horn offers his own body as its case. The boys take the Thunderbird Warbundle and with their followers go on a raid to the other side of the sky.

Hall has shown that the mythic cycle of Red Horn and his sons has some interesting analogies with the Hero Twins mythic cycle of Mesoamerica.

Red Horn had red hair pulled back in a ponytail. Red hair is generally part of the Caucasoid race. Again, we have mention of cannibalistic giants on the other side of the globe.

There are other legends associating Red Horn with a star. He is probably also the source behind the birdman cult throughout the Mississippian people.

There have been 2 main caves discovered with pictographs about Red Horn. One is the Gottschall Site in Wisconsin and the other is Picture Cave in Missouri. Unfortunately one of them was vandalized and has been shut down and closed. No further study can be done on it or presented to the public. According to Wikipedia:

Gottschall Rockshelter (a horizontally shallow cave), located in Muscoda, Wisconsin, contains about forty pictographs. Robert J. Salzer began to excavate the site in 1982, eight years after it had been rediscovered. He identified Panel 5 to be of special interest, since it is a composition containing several figures that seem to be engaged in a single action. Panel 5 is dated with a good measure of confidence to the tenth century A.D. At the outset, Robert L. Hall, the leader in the field, pointed out to Selzer that one of the figures in Panel 5 appeared to have attributes associated with the Red Horn mythology.

The character in your Fig. 4 has a pattern around each nipple which resembles the long-nose god maskettes. The face[s] of the maskettes are of the same outline as that found around each nipple on the pictograph. I first interpreted the two parallel lines above the "face" outline as the red horn. I now feel that they represent the long nose of the long-nosed god in a face-on perspective which the artists could not quite handle. That leaves the nipples for the mouth and tongue, and remember that the little faces stuck out their tongues when manipulated. The stone Big Boy pipe from Spiro had long-nose god maskettes on each ear, and I would guess that is what Red Horn also wore on his ears and was the reason he was called He-who-wears-human-heads-as-earrings.

Salzer identified the other figures as being two giants, one of whom was the woman that eventually married Red Horn, and other pictographs seemed to be of Turtle and Storms-as-He-Walks, all of whom had gathered together on the occasion of the great lacrosse game between the good spirits and the giants. Salzer believes, contrary to Hall, that the figure to the far right is not a son of Red Horn, but Red Horn himself. The reason why we do not see prosopic earpieces is that part of the tail of the bird in the center of the panel has been painted over Red Horn's ears. Most archaeologists have accepted the idea that the panel is devoted to Red Horn mythology, although a few others have been highly skeptical.

Picture Cave

The Red Horn panel from Picture Cave, Missouri.
http://en.wikipedia.org/wiki/File:Image.pict.PictureCaveRH.jpg (pubic domain)

In Warren County, Missouri, there is a site appropriately styled "Picture Cave". As its name suggests, it contains a wealth of pictographs, including one that has been identified with the Hotcąk spirit Red Horn (Wears Faces on His Ears). Other pictographs in Picture Cave have been dated from about 915 AD to 1066 AD, although the age of the "Red Horn" pictograph has so far not been determined. It differs stylistically from the other pictographs in the cave and has a patina of silica which may suggest that it is older than the others. Almost solely on the basis of the prosopic earpiece, Duncan connects the main character of this scene with Red Horn. He describes the chief figure in the panel as "Morning Star (known by the Winnebago as Red Horn)", an identification which has now become universal among archaeologists (see the section above, "Red Horn as a Star"). He also believes that the Red Horn of Picture Cave is carrying the head of Morning Star, which he describes as an act of self-resurrection. Nevertheless, at one point Duncan says, with respect to the "Red Horn" pictograph, "This 'early' Braden style rendering conforms to the description of He-who-wears-human-heads-as-earrings, or Red Horn, after he wrestled with the 'giants'. Red Horn's head is described as being carried by one of his sons ... this is an unmistakable scene at Picture Cave that is finely and delicately rendered and includes a substantial use of white pigment." [26]

The birdman cult is prevalent amongst the ancient Mississippian people, some of the Polynesian people, and probably takes its form as the feathered serpent amongst the Mesoamerican and South American people.

I believe without a doubt that Hare is Zeus and Bird Man is Dionysus-Osiris. Set is probably Red Horn. Now let's take a look at the White Buffalo Woman story. According to Wikipedia:

---

[26] Wikipedia

The traditional story is that, long ago, there was a time of famine. The chief of the Lakotas sent out two scouts to hunt for food. As the young men travelled they saw a figure in the distance. As they approached they saw that it was a beautiful young woman in white clothing. One of the men was filled with desire for the woman. He approached her, telling his companion he would attempt to embrace the woman, and if he found her pleasing, he would claim her as a wife. His companion warned him that she appeared to be a sacred woman, and to do anything sacrilegious would be folly. The man ignored the other's advice.

The companion watched as the other approached and embraced the woman, during which time a white cloud enveloped the pair. After a while, the cloud disappeared and only the mysterious woman and a pile of bones remained. The remaining man was frightened, and began to draw his bow, but the woman beckoned him forward, telling him that no harm would come to him. As the woman spoke Lakota, the young man decided she was one of his people, and came forward. When he arrived, she pointed to a spot on the ground where the other scout's bare bones lay. She explained that the Crazy Buffalo had compelled the man to desire her, and she had annihilated him.

The man became even more frightened and again menaced her with his bow. At this time, the woman explained that she was wakan/holy and his weapons could not harm her. She further explained that if he did as she instructed, no harm would befall him and that his tribe would become more prosperous. The scout promised to do what she instructed, and was told to return to his encampment, call the Council and prepare a feast for her arrival.

The woman's name was *PtesanWi* which translated *White Buffalo Calf Woman*. She taught the Lakotas seve sacred rituals and gave them the chaunupa or sacred pipe which is the holiest of all worship symbols. After teaching the people and giving them her gifts, *PtesanWi* left them promising to return. Later, the story became attributed to the goddess Wohpe, also known as Whope, or Wope.[27]

Could white buffalo woman been one of the daughters of Zeus, such as Athena or Artemis? Additionally, there are stories of red-haired giants all over the Americas. The Pauite have a legend of smoking them to death in a cave in Nevada. Several mummies have been discovered in Lovelock Cave, but many of them have disappeared. Some were even delibertly destroyed.

According to the Paiutes, the Si-Te-Cah were red-haired band of cannibalistic giants. The Si-Te-Cah and the Paiutes were at war, and after a long struggle a coalition of tribes trapped the remaining Si-Te-Cah in Lovelock Cave. When they refused to come out, the Indians piled brush before the cave mouth and set it aflame. The Si-Te-Cah were annihilated.

Sarah Winnemucca Hopkins, daughter of Paiute Chief Winnemucca, related many stories about the Si-Te-Cah in her book Life Among the Piutes: Their Wrongs and Claims. "My people say that the tribe we exterminated had reddish hair. I have some of their hair, which has been handed down from father to son. I have a dress which has been in our family a great many years, trimmed with the reddish hair. I am going to wear it some time when I lecture. It is called a mourning dress, and no one has such a dress but my family."

The Paiute tradition asserts that the Si-Te-Cah people practiced cannibalism, and this may have had some basis in fact. During the 1924 excavation of the cave, a series of three human bones were found near the surface towards the mouth of the cave. "These had been split to extract the marrow, as animal bones were split, and probably indicate cannibalism during a famine.[28]

Per Sarah Winnemuca:

Among the traditions of our people is one of a small tribe of barbarians who used to live along the Humboldt River. It was many hundred years ago. They used

---

[27] Wikipedia
[28] Wikipedia

to waylay my people and kill and eat them. They would dig large holes in our trails at night, and if any of our people travelled at night, which they did, for they were afraid of these barbarous people, they would oftentimes fall into these holes. That tribe would even eat their own dead-yes, they would even come and dig up our dead after they were buried, and would carry them off and eat them. Now and then they would come and make war on my people. They would fight, and as fast as they killed one another on either side, the women would carry off those who were killed. My people say they were very brave. When they were fighting they would jump up in the air after the arrows that went over their heads, and shoot the same arrows back again. My people took some of them into their families, but they could not make them like themselves. So at last they made war on them. This war lasted a long time. Their number was about twenty-six hundred (2600). The war lasted some three years. My people killed them in great numbers, and what few were left went into the thick bush. My people set the bush on fire. This was right above Humboldt Lake. Then they went to work and made tule or bulrush boats, and went into Humboldt Lake. They could not live there very long without fire. They were nearly starving. My people were watching them all round the lake, and would kill them as fast as they would come on land…

This tribe was called people-eaters and after my people had killed them all, the people round us called us Say-do-carah. It means conqueror; its the name of Piutes. It is not an Indian word, I think it is misinterpreted.

My people say that the tribe we exterminated had reddish hair. I have some of their hair, which has been handed down from father to son. I have a dress which has been in our family a great many years, trimmed with this reddish hair.[29]

- Sarah Winnemucca Hopkins, *Life Among the Piutes*, Pages 73-75

The remains of the Sitecah were recovered along with artifacts. A fraternity got a hold of the best adult mummies and destroyed them in a bizarre ceremony. You have to ask yourself

---

[29] Sarah Winnemucca Hopkins, *Life Among the Piutes*, Pages 73-75

why would a fraternity want to do this and why wasn't the find of giant red-haired mummies the find of the century in America.

> **A written report by James H. Hart, the first of two miners to excavate the cave in the fall of 1911, recalls that in the north-central part of the cave, about four feet deep, "was a striking looking body of a man "six feet six inches tall." His body was mummified and his hair distinctly red." Unfortunately in the first year of mining, some of the human remains and artifacts were lost and destroyed. "The best specimen of the adult mummies was boiled and destroyed by a local fraternal lodge, which wanted the skeleton for initiation purposes." Also, several of the fiber sandals found in the cave were remarkably large, and one reported at over 15 inches (38 cm) in length was said to be on display at the Nevada Historical Society's museum in Reno in 1952.[30]**

We know for a fact that the Vikings came to America around 1000 CE and that they tried several times to establish a colony in Vinland. They were chased out. The Vikings were able to settle Greenland and Iceland and they have an oral tradition of the "other people" that they called Skraelings (thin and scrawny) trying to bargain for their weapons in Vinland (America). When they refused, the others tried to steal the weapons and warfare broke out.

There is ample oral tradition that both red-haired people (Vikings and/or Celts) met with Asiatic people in the Americas and in Iceland and Greenland. Each side had bad things to say about the other. In some places in America one group (the red-haired tribe) was wiped out by the other. The biggest question of all is why are the artifacts and skeletal remains being destroyed to hide this history? The Vikings had an end-times story called Ragnarok. In that story, the gods lose to the giants in the end. Perhaps the answer to the question of why the remains and evidence are being destroyed lies with understanding what happened in the past and why "some people" want to cover this up.

All though many Mayan codices were burnt, there appears to be many Aztec codices that survived to tell the tale of the Aztec (Mexica) people. A very interesting story about the Aztec

---

[30] Wikipedia

people leaving their homeland, Aztlan, to escape an over-bearing ruling elite is shown in the Codex Boturini.

http://en.wikipedia.org/wiki/File:Aztlan_codex_boturini.jpg (public domain)

According to Mesoamericans, Queztlcoatl (Viracocha, Kulkulkan) came around disguised as a beggar to check on humans to see if they were still following his teachings. His son also came around and taught civilization to people. According to Wikipedia:

> **Spanish chroniclers from the 16th century claimed that when the conquistadors led by Francisco Pizarro first encountered the Incas they were greeted as Gods, "Viracochas", because their lighter skin resembled their God Viracocha. This story was first reported by Pedro Cieza de León (1553) and later by Pedro Sarmiento de Gamboa. Similar accounts by Spanish chroniclers (e.g. Juan de Betanzos) describe Viracocha as a "White God", often with a beard. The whiteness of Viracocha is however not mentioned in the native authentic legends of the Incas**

and most modern scholars therefore consider the "White God" story to be post-conquest Spanish invention.

Similarly to the Incan god Viracocha, the Aztec god Quetzalcoatl and several other deities from Central and South American pantheons, Bochica is described in legends as being bearded. The beard, once believed to be a mark of a prehistoric European influence and quickly fueled and embellished by spirits of the colonial era, had its single significance in the continentally insular culture of Mesoamerica. The Anales de Cuauhtitlan is a very important early source which is particularly valuable for having been originally written in Nahuatl. The Anales de Cuauhtitlan describes the attire of Quetzalcoatl at Tula:

"Immediately he made him his green mask; he took red color with which he made the lips russet; he took yellow to make the facade; and he made the fangs; continuing, he made his beard of feathers…"

In another legend, Viracocha had two sons, Imahmana Viracocha and Tocapo Virachocha. After the Great Flood and the Creation, Viracocha sent his sons to visit the tribes to the Northeast and Northwest to determine if they still obeyed his commandments. Viracocha himself traveled North. During their journey, Imaymana and Tocapo gave names to all the trees, flowers, fruits, and herbs. They also taught the tribes which of these were edible, which had medicinal properties, and which were poisonous. Eventually, Viracocha, Tocapo and Imahmana arrived at Cuzco (in modern day Peru) and the Pacific seacoast where they walked across the water until they disappeared. The word "Viracocha" literally means "Sea Foam".

The Tarim mummies in China were found recently and are from a tall European race of people that lived in the area. According to Wikipedia:

> **The Tarim mummies are a series of mummies discovered in the Tarim Basin in present-day Xinjiang, China, which date from 1900 BC to 200 AD. Some of the mummies are frequently associated with the presence of the Indo-European Tocharian languages in the Tarim Basin, although the evidence is not totally conclusive.**
>
> **Research into the subject has attracted controversy, due to ethnic tensions in modern day Xinjiang. There have been concerns whether DNA results could affect claims by Uyghur peoples of being indigenous to the region. In comparing the DNA of the mummies to that of modern day Uyghur peoples, Victor H. Mair's team found some genetic similarities with the mummies, but no direct links, stating that "modern DNA and ancient DNA show that Uighurs, Kazaks, Kyrgyzs, the peoples of Central Asia are all mixed Caucasian and East Asian... the modern and ancient DNA tell the same story." He concludes that the mummies are basically Caucasoid, likely speakers of an Indo-European language; that East Asian peoples "began showing up in the eastern portions of the Tarim Basin about 3,000 years ago... while the Uighur peoples arrived after the collapse of the Orkon Uighur Kingdom, largely based in modern day Mongolia, around the year 842.**

One more interesting thing is that the Hawaiians considered the goddess Pele to be a tall white woman with red hair, who was killed by a jealous sister and was buried on an island off of Maui. Per Wikipedia:

> **In one version of the story, Pele is daughter of Kanehoalani and Haumea in the mystical land of Kuaihelani, a floating free land like Fata Morgana. Kuaihelani was in the region of Kahiki (Kukulu o Kahiki). She stays so close to her mother's fireplace with the fire-keeper Lono-makua. Her older sister Nā-maka-o-Kahaʻi, a sea goddess, fears that Pele's ambition would smother the home-land and drives**

Pele away. Kamohoali'i drives Pele south in a canoe called Honua-i-a-kea with her younger sister Hi'iaka and with her brothers Ka-moho-ali'i, Kane-milo-hai, Kane-apua, and arrives at the islets above Hawaii. There Kane-milo-hai is left on Mokupapapa, just a reef, to build it up in fitness for human residence. On Nihoa, 800 feet above the ocean she leaves Kane-apua after her visit to Lehua and crowning a wreath of kau-no'a. Pele feels sorry for her younger brother and picks him up again. Pele used the divining rod, Pa'oa to pick her a new home. A group of chants tells of a pursuit by Namakaokaha'i and Pele is torn apart. Her bones, KaiwioPele form a hill on Kahikinui, while her spirit escaped to the island of Hawaii. (Pele & Hi'iaka A myth from HAwaii by Nathaniel B. Emerson)

Chapter 6

Nordic Mythology, Travels to Vinland, Celtic Mythology, Travels to America

The Nordics are a group of people in Northern Europe that include the ancient Vikings. Generally Nordic countries include Sweden (9 million), Norway (5 million), Finland (5 million), Greenland (56,000), Iceland (320,000), parts of Northern Germany (81 million in Germany) and Denmark (5 million). The Nordics have travelled all over the world, including to the Americas. They also have a rich collection of ancient mythology and legends and include a pantheon of gods and goddesses as well. Many of the ancient myths have been recorded in poetic form in the Poetic Eddas. The Nordic pantheon included gods divided into multiple groups and multiple worlds. The pantheon includes the following gods/goddesses:

Odin - Father of the Gods
Baldr - The son of Odin who was killed
Freyr - God of Fertility
Freyja - Goddess of Fertility
Frigg - Wife of Odin, Mother of Baldr
Loki - Trickster God
Thor - God of Thunder
Tyr - God of War
Ve - Brother of Odin
Villi - Brother of Odin

There are many other Nordic gods and goddesses, but these are the main gods and goddesses of the Nordics. The dragon was an important symbol as well as the evergreen tree to the Nordics

According to Nordic traditions, the beginning of the universe began with fire and ice. There were only two worlds at the time, Muspelheim and Niflheim. When the warm air of Muspelheim touched the cold ice of Niflheim, a giant named Ymir and an icy cow named Audhumla were created. A son came from Ymir's foot and a man and a woman came from Ymir's armpits. This man and woman were the Jotun or the giants. From Ymir and the cow came Buri. And from Buri and a giantess came a male named Bor. Bor became the father of the three gods Odin, Vili and Ve. These three gods created humans.

The Universe is held up by a great ash tree called Yggdrasil. It comes from one of Odin's names, Yggr. Around the tree, there are nine worlds. The world serpent is coiled around the roots of the tree. There are seven worlds in the roots. They are Muspelsheim, Land of Raging Fire; Svartalfheim, land of the dwarves; Hel, land of the Dead; Niflheim, land of Ice and Mist; Jotunheim, land of the frost giants; Vanaheim, land of the Vanir; and Alfheim, land of the elves. The dragon Nidhoggr constantly naws at the roots holding Niflheim. Niflheim is the underworld and is a land of snow and ice. The upper world, at the top of the tree, is called the Asgard and this is the home of the gods. Valhalla is a hall of warriors who have died bravely and are allowed to feast and drink there for all eternity. Humans live in the Midgard or the middle of the tree. The human world is surrounded by a sea of monsters, but we are linked to the Asgard by a rainbow bridge. Odin is the father God and is wisest amongst all the gods. He rides across the sky on Sleipnir, which we know is his grey eight-legged horse. A pair of wolves ride with him and his two ravens that sit on his shoulder fly across the world and come back and report to him all that they have seen. The valkyries are servants that attend to the gods.

Skaldas told the history of the Nordics. It is said that Odin hung on this tree by one foot for nine days. After this ordeal, he received the sacred 24 runes and nine powerful songs. Odin said,

I know that I hung on a windy tree
nine long nights,
wounded with a spear, dedicated to Odin,
myself to myself,
on that tree of which no man knows

from where its roots run.[31]

The first humans were called Ask and Embla and they originated from Yggdrasil. Ragnarok is the final destiny of the Gods.

At the time of Ragnarok, it is said that man will become evil. Brothers will fight brothers and no one will care about their kinship. The world will go through an ax age, a sword age, a wind age and a wolf age before it enters into Ragnarok. There will be no kindness or mercy.

Various natural disasters will take place. The land will be submerged into the water. And a final battle of the Gods will take place and the dead will walk the Earth

Odin will fight the wolf Fenrir and be killed by him. Freyr will fight Surtr. Vidar will avenge Odin by killing Fenrir. Thor will fight the serpent and defeat it, but will collapse afterwards. After the war, the sun will become black and the earth will sink into the sea. The stars will vanish and the flames will touch the sky.

After all of this, the earth will reappear from the water. The surviving Gods will meet together. Some Gods will be reborn. They will talk about the games the old Gods used to play and the grass will grow again. Humans will descend from Lif and Lifthrasir, who will be the only surviving humans, after Ragnarok. The Gods and the humans will live together in peace. Wickedness and evil will no longer exist. I personally believe Ragnarok has already happened. Here again, mythology divides time up into ages just like the Greeks and Egyptians. I also believe the great flood was the rising of the ocean floor by 300 feet which wiped out many coastal cities.

According to wikipedia:

The *Poetic Edda* is a collection of Old Norse poems primarily preserved in the Icelandic mediaeval manuscript Code Regius. Along with Snorri Sturluson's *Prose Edda*, the *Poetic Edda* is the most important extant source on Norse mythology and Germanic heroic legends, and from the early 19th century onwards has had a

---

[31] Wikipedia

powerful influence on later Scandinavian literatures, not merely through the stories it contains but through the visionary force and dramatic quality of many of the poems.

Here is the text from the Poetic Edda's first book, the Voluspa:

1. Hearing I ask | from the holy races,
From Heimdall's sons, | both high and low;
Thou wilt, Valfather, | that well I relate
Old tales I remember | of men long ago.
2. I remember yet | the giants of yore,
Who gave me bread | in the days gone by;
Nine worlds I knew, | the nine in the tree
With mighty roots | beneath the mold.
3. Of old was the age | when Ymir lived;
Sea nor cool waves | nor sand there were;
Earth had not been, | nor heaven above,
But a yawning gap, | and grass nowhere.
4. Then Bur's sons lifted | the level land,
Mithgarth the mighty | there they made;
The sun from the south | warmed the stones of earth,
And green was the ground | with growing leeks.
5. The sun, the sister | of the moon, from the south
Her right hand cast | over heaven's rim;
No knowledge she had | where her home should be,
The moon knew not | what might was his,

6. Then sought the gods | their assembly-seats,
The holy ones, | and council held;

Names then gave they | to noon and twilight,

Morning they named, | and the waning moon,

Night and evening, | the years to number.

7. At Ithavoll met | the mighty gods,

Shrines and temples | they timbered high;

Forges they set, and | they smithied ore,

Tongs they wrought, | and tools they fashioned.

8. In their dwellings at peace | they played at tables,

Of gold no lack | did the gods then know,--

Till thither came | up giant-maids three,

Huge of might, | out of Jotunheim.

9. Then sought the gods | their assembly-seats,

The holy ones, | and council held,

To find who should raise | the race of dwarfs

Out of Brimir's blood | and the legs of Blain.

10. There was Motsognir | the mightiest made

Of all the dwarfs, | and Durin next;

Many a likeness | of men they made,

The dwarfs in the earth, | as Durin said.

11. Nyi and Nithi, | Northri and Suthri,

Austri and Vestri, | Althjof, Dvalin,

Nar and Nain, | Niping, Dain,

Bifur, Bofur, | Bombur, Nori,

An and Onar, | Ai, Mjothvitnir.

12. Vigg and Gandalf) | Vindalf, Thrain,

Thekk and Thorin, | Thror, Vit and Lit,

Nyr and Nyrath,-- | now have I told--

Regin and Rathsvith-- | the list aright.

13. Fili, Kili, | Fundin, Nali,

Heptifili, | Hannar, Sviur,

Frar, Hornbori, | Fræg and Loni,

Aurvang, Jari, | Eikinskjaldi.

14. The race of the dwarfs | in Dvalin's throng

Down to Lofar | the list must I tell;

The rocks they left, | and through wet lands

They sought a home | in the fields of sand.

15. There were Draupnir | and Dolgthrasir,

Hor, Haugspori, | Hlevang, Gloin,

Dori, Ori, | Duf, Andvari,

Skirfir, Virfir, | Skafith, Ai.

16. Alf and Yngvi, | Eikinskjaldi,

Fjalar and Frosti, | Fith and Ginnar;

So for all time | shall the tale be known,

The list of all | the forbears of Lofar.

17. Then from the throng | did three come forth,

From the home of the gods, | the mighty and gracious;

Two without fate | on the land they found,

Ask and Embla, | empty of might.

18. Soul they had not, | sense they had not,

Heat nor motion, | nor goodly hue;

Soul gave Othin, | sense gave Hönir,

Heat gave Lothur | and goodly hue.

19. An ash I know, | Yggdrasil its name,

With water white | is the great tree wet;

Thence come the dews | that fall in the dales,

Green by Urth's well | does it ever grow.

20. Thence come the maidens | mighty in wisdom,

Three from the dwelling | down 'neath the tree;

Urth is one named, | Verthandi the next,--

On the wood they scored,-- | and Skuld the third.

Laws they made there, and life allotted

To the sons of men, and set their fates.

21. The war I remember, | the first in the world,

When the gods with spears | had smitten Gollveig,

And in the hall | of Hor had burned her,

Three times burned, | and three times born,

Oft and again, | yet ever she lives.

22. Heith they named her | who sought their home,

The wide-seeing witch, | in magic wise;

Minds she bewitched | that were moved by her magic,

To evil women | a joy she was.

23. On the host his spear | did Othin hurl,

Then in the world | did war first come;

The wall that girdled | the gods was broken,

And the field by the warlike | Wanes was trodden.

24. Then sought the gods | their assembly-seats,

The holy ones, | and council held,

Whether the gods | should tribute give,

Or to all alike | should worship belong.

25. Then sought the gods | their assembly-seats,

The holy ones, | and council held,

To find who with venom | the air had filled,

Or had given Oth's bride | to the giants' brood.

26. In swelling rage | then rose up Thor,--

Seldom he sits | when he such things hears,--

And the oaths were broken, | the words and bonds,

The mighty pledges | between them made.

27. I know of the horn | of Heimdall, hidden

Under the high-reaching | holy tree;

On it there pours | from Valfather's pledge

A mighty stream: | would you know yet more?

28. Alone I sat | when the Old One sought me,

The terror of gods, | and gazed in mine eyes:

"What hast thou to ask? | why comest thou hither?

Othin, I know | where thine eye is hidden."

29. I know where Othin's | eye is hidden,

Deep in the wide-famed | well of Mimir;

Mead from the pledge | of Othin each morn

Does Mimir drink: | would you know yet more?

30. Necklaces had I | and rings from Heerfather,

Wise was my speech | and my magic wisdom;

. . . .

Widely I saw | over all the worlds.

31. On all sides saw I | Valkyries assemble,

Ready to ride | to the ranks of the gods;

Skuld bore the shield, | and Skogul rode next,

Guth, Hild, Gondul, | and Geirskogul.

Of Herjan's maidens | the list have ye heard,

Valkyries ready | to ride o'er the earth.

32. I saw for Baldr, | the bleeding god,

The son of Othin, | his destiny set:

Famous and fair | in the lofty fields,

Full grown in strength | the mistletoe stood.

33. From the branch which seemed | so slender and fair

Came a harmful shaft | that Hoth should hurl;

But the brother of Baldr | was born ere long,

And one night old | fought Othin's son.

34. His hands he washed not, | his hair he combed not,

Till he bore to the bale-blaze | Baldr's foe.

But in Fensalir | did Frigg weep sore

For Valhall's need: | would you know yet more?

35. One did I see | in the wet woods bound,

A lover of ill, | and to Loki like;

By his side does Sigyn | sit, nor is glad

To see her mate: | would you know yet more?

36. From the east there pours | through poisoned vales

With swords and daggers | the river Slith.

. . . .

. . . .

37. Northward a hall | in Nithavellir

Of gold there rose | for Sindri's race;

And in Okolnir | another stood,

Where the giant Brimir | his beer-hall had.

38. A hall I saw, | far from the sun,

On Nastrond it stands, | and the doors face north,

Venom drops | through the smoke-vent down,

For around the walls | do serpents wind.

39. I saw there wading | through rivers wild

Treacherous men | and murderers too,

And workers of ill | with the wives of men;

There Nithhogg sucked | the blood of the slain,

And the wolf tore men; | would you know yet more?

40. The giantess old | in Ironwood sat,

In the east, and bore | the brood of Fenrir;

Among these one | in monster's guise

Was soon to steal | the sun from the sky.

41. There feeds he full | on the flesh of the dead,

And the home of the gods | he reddens with gore;

Dark grows the sun, | and in summer soon
Come mighty storms: | would you know yet more?

42. On a hill there sat, | and smote on his harp,
Eggther the joyous, | the giants' warder;
Above him the cock | in the bird-wood crowed,
Fair and red | did Fjalar stand.

43. Then to the gods | crowed Gollinkambi,
He wakes the heroes | in Othin's hall;
And beneath the earth | does another crow,
The rust-red bird | at the bars of Hel.

44. Now Garm howls loud | before Gnipahellir,
The fetters will burst, | and the wolf run free;
Much do I know, | and more can see
Of the fate of the gods, | the mighty in fight.

45. Brothers shall fight | and fell each other,
And sisters' sons | shall kinship stain;
Hard is it on earth, | with mighty whoredom;
Axe-time, sword-time, | shields are sundered,
Wind-time, wolf-time, | ere the world falls;
Nor ever shall men | each other spare.

46. Fast move the sons | of Mim, and fate
Is heard in the note | of the Gjallarhorn;
Loud blows Heimdall, | the horn is aloft,
In fear quake all | who on Hel-roads are.

47. Yggdrasil shakes, | and shiver on high
The ancient limbs, | and the giant is loose;
To the head of Mim | does Othin give heed,
But the kinsman of Surt | shall slay him soon.

48. How fare the gods? | how fare the elves?
All Jotunheim groans, | the gods are at council;

Loud roar the dwarfs | by the doors of stone,

The masters of the rocks: | would you know yet more?

49. Now Garm howls loud | before Gnipahellir,

The fetters will burst, | and the wolf run free

Much do I know, | and more can see

Of the fate of the gods, | the mighty in fight.

50. From the east comes Hrym | with shield held high;

In giant-wrath | does the serpent writhe;

O'er the waves he twists, | and the tawny eagle

Gnaws corpses screaming; | Naglfar is loose.

51. O'er the sea from the north | there sails a ship

With the people of Hel, | at the helm stands Loki;

After the wolf | do wild men follow,

And with them the brother | of Byleist goes.

52. Surt fares from the south | with the scourge of branches,

The sun of the battle-gods | shone from his sword;

The crags are sundered, | the giant-women sink,

The dead throng Hel-way, | and heaven is cloven.

53. Now comes to Hlin | yet another hurt,

When Othin fares | to fight with the wolf,

And Beli's fair slayer | seeks out Surt,

For there must fall | the joy of Frigg.

54. Then comes Sigfather's | mighty son,

Vithar, to fight | with the foaming wolf;

In the giant's son | does he thrust his sword

Full to the heart: | his father is avenged.

55. Hither there comes | the son of Hlothyn,

The bright snake gapes | to heaven above;

. . . .

Against the serpent | goes Othin's son.

56. In anger smites | the warder of earth,--

Forth from their homes | must all men flee;-

Nine paces fares | the son of Fjorgyn,

And, slain by the serpent, | fearless he sinks.

57. The sun turns black, | earth sinks in the sea,

The hot stars down | from heaven are whirled;

Fierce grows the steam | and the life-feeding flame,

Till fire leaps high | about heaven itself.

58. Now Garm howls loud | before Gnipahellir,

The fetters will burst, | and the wolf run free;

Much do I know, | and more can see

Of the fate of the gods, | the mighty in fight.

59. Now do I see | the earth anew

Rise all green | from the waves again;

The cataracts fall, | and the eagle flies,

And fish he catches | beneath the cliffs.

60. The gods in Ithavoll | meet together,

Of the terrible girdler | of earth they talk,

And the mighty past | they call to mind,

And the ancient runes | of the Ruler of Gods.

61. In wondrous beauty | once again

Shall the golden tables | stand mid the grass,

Which the gods had owned | in the days of old,

. . . .

62. Then fields unsowed | bear ripened fruit,

All ills grow better, | and Baldr comes back;

Baldr and Hoth dwell | in Hropt's battle-hall,

And the mighty gods: | would you know yet more?

63. Then Hönir wins | the prophetic wand,

. . . .

And the sons of the brothers | of Tveggi abide
In Vindheim now: | would you know yet more?
64. More fair than the sun, | a hall I see,
Roofed with gold, | on Gimle it stands;
There shall the righteous | rulers dwell,
And happiness ever | there shall they have.
65. There comes on high, | all power to hold,
A mighty lord, | all lands he rules.

. . . .
. . . .

66. From below the dragon | dark comes forth,
Nithhogg flying | from Nithafjoll;
The bodies of men on | his wings he bears,
The serpent bright: | but now must I sink.[32]

 Eric the Red was a famous warrior. But he got in trouble for killing two fellow Vikings and was banished to Iceland from Norway around 982. He went there and then took a trip out in the water to see if there was any more land. He found Greenland and started a settlement there. He had a son that was called Leif Erickson. The last name of a Viking child is the first name of the father and the word son afterwards if it is a boy. Leif Erickson grew up and decided to journey even further on the water when he discovered the new land. He called it Vinland because of the grapes he found. The Vikings called the native people in Iceland and Greenland, skraeling. It meant "weaklings". They called the people they met in Vinland, the same thing.

 After Leif returned with his stories, his brother Thorvald decided to visit and explore the new Vinland. He took a crew of about thirty and sailed to Vinland. He stayed over the winter and decided to explore in the spring. Unfortunately, a fight broke out between the natives and the Vikings and several natives were killed. The Vikings were outnumbered. When they were sleeping, they heard a voice telling them to wake up and get out of the land as fast as they could.

---

[32] Henry Adams Bellow, *The Poetic Edda*, pages 1-27.

They tried to, but were attacked by the natives with arrows. The Vikings didn't fight back, but concentrated on escaping. Once they were out to sea, Thorvald realized he had been hit with an arrow. The crew sailed up the land where they had stayed before and Thorvald died and was buried there. The crew gathered some food and headed back to Greenland.

Leif Erickson's other brother, Thorstein decided to sail to Vinland, next. He and his crew had a rough time getting there, but made it to the first settlement. Unfortunately, an illness swept through and Thorstein died. The survivors sailed back to Greenland, in the spring.

Another Viking named Karlsefni, who ended up marrying Thorstein's widow, decided to take a trip to Vinland. They went, settled in at the first camp and got through a winter. But the next summer, the natives came and investigated the camp of the Vikings. The natives wanted to trade for weapons, but the Vikings said no. But they did trade some food with the natives. But the natives wanted the weapons and tried to steal them. This led to more fighting. The Vikings won, but felt uneasy about staying in Vinland. They gathered up supplies and food and sailed back to Greenland.

The last trip to Vinland was the one with Leif's sister, Freydis and her husband. She gathered up a group and sailed to Vinland. Fights broke out with the Viking settlers in Vinland, which led to bloodshed. Two men had moved into the Erickson's house in Vinland and Freydis argued about it, until things led to the death of the men and their supporters. The survivors waited till the spring to sail back to Greenland.

The Celts were a people who lived all over Europe, including Germany, Spain, France, England, and Ireland. They had their own language and their own mythologies and legends. Today, most of Celtic lore comes from Ireland. The Irish Cycles include 4 major time periods from the time of the ancient gods to the last kings of Ireland. Celtic mythology is also rich in stories of giants and little people. The main gods/goddesses of the Irish Celts are the following:

Daghda - Leader of the Gods
The Morrigan - A Triple Battle Goddess
Lugh/Lug - Ancient God King
Brigid - Dagda's Daughter
Epona - Goddess of Horses

Nuada - Ancient God King
Goibniu - Smith of the Gods
Mananna Mac Lir - God of the Sea
Dian Cecht - God of Medicine

Other Celtic people such as the Welsh and the Gaels, have their own names for their gods/goddesses. Gaelic people used a script called Ogham to record their myths. The Irish didn't have many of their myths recorded until after the arrival of Christianity. Druids known as Bards would sing the history of ancient Ireland from generation to generation. This is how they preserved their history.

The Celts grew grains, vegetables and fruit. They ate breads and stews and drank mead. Bards were the poets who sang songs of the history of the people and often sang during festivals. The women wore long dresses and the men wore shirts and tunics. The women wore their hair back in combs or in braids. The men were tall and strong. They had music and crafts and inventions. They had use of the wheel for their chariots and they had ships to travel across the waters. They buried their dead in burial mounds and also made effigies of animals and symbols in the grass that can still be seen today.

The Tuatha De DaNaan battled the sea gods called the Fomorians for the land. The Tuatha De DaNaan had created humans and the giants of the sea were jealous. They vowed to defeat the gods and goddesses and take the land and humans for themselves. They lost after a great battle and Tuatha Danaan won after much destruction. However, there were Fomorians that had survived the war

The holidays celebrated by the Celts included Imbolc in February for the coming of spring. Beltane for the beginning of summer in May, Lughnassadh in August for the coming of fall and Samhain in November as the beginning of winter, the vernal equinox on March 21 and the autumnal equinox on September 21, and the summer solstice on June 21 and the winter solstice on December 21 are also celebrated.

According to Wikipedia:

The first known text that describes the druids is Julius Caesar's *Commentarii de Bello Gallico*, book VI, written in the 50s or 40s BCE. A military general who was intent on conquering Gaul and Britain, Caesar described the druids as being concerned with "divine worship, the due performance of sacrifices, private or public, and the interpretation of ritual questions." He claimed that they played an important part in Gaulish society, being one of the two respected classes along with the *equites* (a term meaning 'horsemen' which has been usually interpreted as referring to warriors) and that they performed the function of judges. He claimed that they recognized the authority of a single leader, who would rule until his death, when a successor would be chosen by vote or through conflict. He also remarked that they met annually at a sacred place in the region occupied by the Carnute tribe in Gaul, while they viewed Britain as the centre of druidic study; and that they were not found amongst the German tribes to the east of the Rhine. According to Caesar, many young men were trained to be druids, during which time they had to learn all the associated lore by heart. He also claimed their main teaching was "the souls do not perish, but after death pass from one to another". They were also concerned with "the stars and their movements, the size of the cosmos and the earth, the world of nature, and the powers of deities", indicating they were involved with not only such common aspects of religion as theology and cosmology, but also astronomy. Caesar also held that they were "administrators" during rituals of human sacrifice, for which criminals were usually used, and that the method was through burning in a wicker man.[33]

The source of the mythological tradition in Ireland is the eleventh-century compilation known as the Leabhar Gabhala or the Book of Invasions.

The Celts also sailed to America long ago. A famous man named Brendan the Navigator, was born in Ireland. He had heard stories about land to the west, from his nephew, and he built a boat and sailed with a few friends across the sea. The boat was built to be carried by the sea currents. He ended up sailing north. He went past an island that had sheep and birds and he

---

[33] Wikipedia

passed islands with ice. He even passed an island of giants who started throwing hot coals at him and his men. As Brendan and his friends continued, they were even attacked by a huge lion-bird called a griffin. But a little bird came and pecked the griffin's eyes to make it leave the men alone. They were attacked by a sea monster that was stopped by another good sea monster from eating the men. The Irish also have tales of giants and little people. The tale of Finn MacCool is a popular one. I hope you have noticed the similarity between the Celtic, Nordic and Greek mythologies. Julius Caesar certainly did as well as other Roman scholars. Julius Caser equated the five great gods of the Celts with the five great god of the Romans: Hermes, Apollo, Mars, Jupiter, and Minerva.

Chapter 7

Egyptian Mythology

Egypt was divided into two kingdoms. One for Horus (lower Egypt) and one for Set (upper Egypt). The two kingdoms were united under Menes about 5200 years ago.

Worship of the gods and goddesses was important and all of the pharaohs and queens claimed ancestry to the gods and goddesses. Egypt was formed by Isis an Osiris and some ancient texts say cities in Egypt were founded by other gods before them.

The worship of gods was divided into sets of threes. The trinity of Osiris, Isis, and Horus was one such trinity. Other multiple of triads included the group of 9 known as Ennead. The Ennead included the god Atum, his children Shu and Tefnut, their children Geb and Nut and their children Osiris, Isis, Set and Nephthys. Geb would be the equivalent of Zeus. Shu an Tefnut would be the equivalent of Cronus and Rhea. Atum is the equivalent of Ouranus. The Ennead was worshipped in the city of the sun known as Heliopolis.

Another group of gods, known as the Ogdoad was worshipped at Hermopolis. The Ogdoad consisted of eight deities worshipped in Hermopolis during what is called the Old Kingdom, the third through sixth dynasties, dated between 2686 to 2134 BC. According to Wikipedia:

> **The eight deities were arranged in four female-male pairs: Naunet and Nu, Amaunet and Amun, Kauket and Kuk, Hauhet and Huh. The females were associated with snakes and the males were associated with frogs. Apart from their gender, there was little to distinguish the female goddess from the male god in a pair; indeed, the names of the females are merely the female forms of the male name and vice versa. Essentially, each pair represents the female and male aspect of one of four concepts, namely the primordial waters (Naunet and Nu), air or invisibility**

(Amunet and Amun), darkness (Kauket and Kuk), and eternity or infinite space (Hauhet and Huh).

Together the four concepts represent the primal, fundamental state of the beginning, they are what always was. In the myth, however, their interaction ultimately proved to be unbalanced, resulting in the arising of a new entity. When the entity opened, it revealed Ra, the fiery sun, inside. After a long interval of rest, Ra, together with the other deities, created all other things.

There are two main variations on the nature of the entity containing Ra:

Egg variant

One version of the myth has the entity arising from the waters after the interaction as a mound of dirt. In the myth an egg was laid upon this mound by a celestial bird. The egg contained Ra. In some variants, the egg is laid by a cosmic goose. However, the egg was also said to have been a gift from Thoth, and laid by an ibis, the bird with which he was associated.

Lotus variant

Later, when Atum had become assimilated into Ra as *Atum-Ra*, the belief that Atum emerged from a (blue) lotus bud, in the Ennead cosmogony, was adopted and attached to Ra. The lotus was said to have arisen from the waters after the explosive interaction as a bud, which floated on the surface, and slowly opened its petals to reveal the beetle, Khepri, inside. Khepri, an aspect of Ra representing the rising sun, immediately turns into a weeping boy – Nefertum, whose tears form the creatures of the earth.[34]

These pairs sound like some of the titans of old to me. Geb and Nut were the parents of Osiris, Isis, Set, and Nephthys. According to Wikipedia:

---

[34] Wikipedia

The oldest representation in a fragmentary relief of the god, was as an anthropomorphic bearded being accompanied by his name, and dating from king Djoser's reign, 3rd Dynasty, and was found in Heliopolis. In later times he could also be depicted as a ram, a bull or a crocodile (the latter in a vignet of the Book of the Dead - papyrus of the lady Heryweben in the Egyptian Museum, Cairo).

Frequently described mythologically as father of snakes (one of the names for snake was *s3-t3* - 'son of the earth' and in a Coffin Texts-spell Geb was described as father of the snake Nehebkau, while his mother was in that case Neith) and therefore depicted sometimes as such. In mythology Geb also often occurs as a primeval divine king of Egypt from whom his son Osiris and his grandson Horus inherited the land after many contendings with the disruptive god Set, brother and killer of Osiris. Geb could also be regarded as personified fertile earth and barren desert, the latter containing the dead or setting them free from their tombs, metaphorically described as 'Geb opening his jaws', or imprisoning those there not worthy to go to the fertile North-Eastern heavenly *Field of Reeds*. In the latter case, one of his otherworldly attributes was an ominous jackal-headed stave (called *wsr.t*) rising from the ground unto which enemies could be bound.[35]

The story of Osiris and his murder was a major story in Egypt. Set set up a dinner party and created an elaborate box and promised it to anyone who fit in it perfectly. Everyone tried it out and when Osiris layed in it, the 72 conspirators sealed up the box and dumped him in the river. His wife Isis searched for his body and found it and buried him. Set found the body and chopped it up into pieces. Isis found all of the pieces except the male organ. She created the obelisk as a tribute to Osiris' male organ.

Horus grew up and avenged his father by defeating Set in a series of competitions and battles. His left eye was damaged in the process. There are writings about Isis and her instructions to the priests on the worship and ways of Osiris in the ancient Greek writings, as well.

---

[35] Wikipedia

Another interesting story of Egypt involves the Hyksos. Egypt had been invaded by the Hyksos who took over the Egyptian lands and enslaved everyone. After a thirty year war, Ahmose I, drove them out. The kingdom belonged to the Princes of Thebes, not to the invading Hyksos. The original Egypt was divided into 2 kingdoms (per the decision of Geb the father god), called Upper and Lower Egypt. The two kingdoms were combined after King Menes (Scorpion) united the kingdoms.

According to Wikipedia:

> **The conflict between the local kings of Thebes and the Hyksos king Apepi had started during the reign of Seqenenre Tao and would be concluded, after almost 30 years of intermittent conflict and war, under the reign of Ahmose I. Seqenenre Tao was possibly killed in a battle against the Hyksos, as his much-wounded mummy gruesomely suggests, and his successor Kamose (likely Ahmose's elder brother) is known to have attacked and raided the lands around the Hyksos capital, Avaris (modern Tell el-Dab'a). Kamose evidently had a short reign, as his highest attested regnal year is year 3, and was succeeded by Ahmose I. Apepi may have died near the same time. The two royal names—Awoserre and Aqenienre—known for Apepi attested in the historical record were for the same Hyksos king that were used by Ahmose's opponent at different times during the latter king's reign.**

This event is the real Exodus spoken about in the bible. The Tempest Stele also describes incredible storms that came through Egypt at the same time. Per Wikipedia:

> **The Tempest Stele (alt. Storm Stele) was erected by Ahmose I early in the eighteenth dynasty of Egypt, *circa* 1550 BCE. The stele describes a great storm striking Egypt during this time, destroying tombs, temples and pyramids in the Theban region and the work of restoration ordered by the king.**

Ahmose I was part of the eighteenth dynasty of Egypt which included very famous pharaohs such as Akhenaten, Thutmose, and Hatshepsut. According to Wikipedia, the Hyksos dynasty didn't last too long and came out of ancient Babylon known as the fertile crescent and they appeared to have only five kings:

The Fifteenth Dynasty arose from among the Hyksos people who emerged out of the Fertile Crescent to establish a short-lived governance over much of the Nile region, and ruled from 1674 to 1535 BC.

The following excerpt from wikipedia describes the Hyksos invaders:

The Hyksos or Hycsos (pron.: /ˈhɪksɒs/; Egyptian *heqa khasewet*, "foreign rulers"; Greek Ὑκσώς, Ὑξώς) were a mixed people from West Asia who took over the eastern Nile Delta, ending the thirteenth dynasty, and initiating the Second Intermediate Period of Ancient Egypt.

The Hyksos first appeared in Egypt c.1800 BC, during the eleventh dynasty, and began their climb to power in the thirteenth dynasty, coming out of the second intermediate period in control of Avaris and the Delta. By the fifteenth dynasty, they ruled Lower Egypt, and at the end of the seventeenth dynasty, they were expelled (c.1560 BC).

The Hyksos practiced horse burials, and their chief deity became the Egyptian storm and desert god, Seth, whom they identified with their native storm god. Although most Hyksos names seem Semitic, the Hyksos also included Hurrians, who, while speaking an isolated language, were under the rule and influence of Indo-Europeans.

The Hyksos brought several technical improvements to Egypt, as well as cultural impulses such as new musical instruments and foreign loan words. The changes affected techniques from bronze working and pottery to weaving, and new breeds of animals and new crops were introduced. In warfare, they introduced the

horse and chariot, the compound bow, improved battle axes, and advanced fortification techniques.

Modern scholarship usually assumes that the Hyksos were likely Semites who came from the Levant. Kamose, the last king of the Theban 17th Dynasty, refers to Apophis as a "Chieftain of Retjenu (i.e., Canaan)" in a stela that implies a Semitic Canaanite background for this Hyksos king: this is the strongest evidence for a Canaanite background for the Hyksos. Khyan's name "has generally been interpreted as Amorite "Hayanu" (reading *h-ya-a-n*) which the Egyptian form represents perfectly, and this is in all likelihood the correct interpretation." Kim Ryholt furthermore observes the name Hayanu is recorded in the Assyrian king-lists for a "remote ancestor" of Shamshi-Adad I (c. 1813 BC) of Assyria, which suggests that it had been used for centuries prior to Khyan's own reign.

According to Wikipedia the Hyksos were kicked out of Egypt and pushed into Canaan.

Chapter 8

Hinduism

Hinduism is a very old religion that is from India. They have 330 million gods/goddesses and many stories of heroes and ancient wars. Tales of giants and little people and serpent people are abundant in Hinduism. Even more interesting are the stories of sophisticated weaponry and flying craft in the ancient Vedic texts. According to wikipedia:

> **Hinduism is the predominant religion of the Indian subcontinent, and one of its indigenous religions. Hinduism includes Shaivism, Vaishnavism and Śrauta among numerous other traditions. It also includes historical groups, for example the Kapalikas. Among other practices and philosophies, Hinduism includes a wide spectrum of laws and prescriptions of "daily morality" based on the notion of karma, dharma, and societal norms. Hinduism is a conglomeration of distinct intellectual or philosophical points of view, rather than a rigid common set of beliefs.**
>
> **Hinduism is formed of diverse traditions and has no single founder Among its direct roots is the historical Vedic religion of Iron Age India and, as such, Hinduism is often called the "oldest living religion"or the "oldest living major religion" in the world.**
>
> **One orthodox classification of Hindu texts is to divide into Śruti ("revealed") and Smrit ("remembered") texts. These texts discuss theology, philosophy, mythology, rituals and temple building among other topics. Major scriptures include the** *Vedas, Upanishads, Purāṇas, Mahābhārata, Rāmāyaṇa, Bhagavad Gītā* **and** *Āgamas.*

Hinduism, with about one billion followers, is the world's third largest religion, after Christianity and Islam.

Some of the main deities of Hinduism are:

Shiva - The Destroyer and Creator of Worlds
Vishnu - The God of Protection and the Preserver
Brahma - The Father God
Kali - The Mother Goddess of War and Death
Parvati - The wife of Shiva
Lakshmi - The wife of Vishnu
Surya - The Sun God
Ganesh - The God of Writing
Varuna - The God of the Ocean
Kubera - The God of Wealth
Krishna - God of Love

    A Vimana is a flying ship in ancient Hindu texts. Vishnu is one of the 3 main gods of Hinduism. He is considered the preserver and maintainer whereas Shiva is considered the destroyer and transformer and Brahma is the creator. Vishnu has come in the form of nine out of ten different avatars at different times. The most famous are Rama and Krishna. His wife is the goddess Lakshmi. Vishnu has already come in his form as nine of the ten avatars and he is yet to come in his tenth avatar form

    Depending on which Purana or vedic writing you read, the gods Brahma, Vishnu, and Shiva are all aspects of one another. The blue skin represents his all pervasive presence in space as well as the water. According to wikipedia, here are his ten avatars:

There are ten avatars (*dashavatara*) of Vishnu commonly considered as the most prominent:

1. Matsya, the fish that kills Damanaka to save the vedas and saves mankind.
2. Kurma, the turtle that helps the Devas and Asuras churn the ocean for the nectar of immortality.
3. Varaha, the boar that rescues the Earth and kills Hiranyaksha.
4. Narasimha, the one (half-Lion half- human) who defeats the demon Hiranyakashapu (Nara = man, simha = lion).
5. Vamana. the dwarf that grows into a giant to save the world from King Bali.
6. Parashurama, A Sage, Rama with the axe, who appeared in the Treta Yuga.
7. Rama, Sri Ramachandra, the prince and king of Ayodhya and killed Demon King Raavana.
8. Krishna (meaning 'dark coloured' or 'all attractive' or the Existence of Bliss,), appeared in the Dwapara Yuga along with his brother
9. Buddha, ((North India) Buddha, the ascetic prince is listed as an avatar of Vishnu in many Hindu scriptures including Bhagavata Purana, Bhavishya Purana, Narasimha Purana etc.[8][9] With the departure of Krishna, Kali Yuga sets in, in this age, the true devotion to Vedas was replaced by empty rituals. To enlighten the world in such times, Vishnu descended the earth as Buddha, the enlightened one.)
10. Kalki ("Eternity", or "timeless", destroyer of time or "The Destroyer of foulness"), who is expected to appear at the end of Kali Yuga, the time period in which we currently exist.

Other writings indicate additional avatars for Vishnu. Vishnu will originate from different forms of the goddess Devi Ma. There was also another ancient god in Hinduism called Indra. Indra looks to be the equivalent of Zeus and he is described as having blonde hair. Per Wikipedia:

Indra, also known as Śakra in the Vedas, is the leader of the Devas or gods and the lord of Svargaloka or heaven in the Hindu religion. He is the god of rain and thunderstorms. He wields a lightning thunderbolt known as *vajra* and rides on a white elephant known as Airavata. Indra is one of the chief deities and is the twin brother of Agni, said to be born of *Dyaus Pitar* (Father Heaven) and *Prithvi Mata* (Mother Earth). He is also mentioned as an Aditya, son of Aditi. His home is situated on Mount Meru in the heaven. He has many epithets, notably *vṛṣan* the bull, and *vṛtrahan*, slayer of Vṛtra, *Meghavahana* "the one who rides the clouds" and *Devapati* "the lord of gods or devas".[3] Indra appears as the name of a Daeva in the Zoroastrian religion, while his epithet Verethragna appears as a god of victory. Indra is also called Śakra frequently in the Vedas and in Buddhism (Pali: *Sakka*).

He is celebrated as a demiurge who pushes up the sky, releases Ushas (dawn) from the Vala cave, and slays Vṛtra; both latter actions are central to the Soma sacrifice. He is associated with Vajrapani - the Chief Dharmapala or Defender and Protector of the Buddha, Dharma and Sangha who embodies the power of all primordial or Dhyani Buddhas. On the other hand, he also commits many kinds of mischief (kilbiṣa) for which he is sometimes punished. In Puranic mythology, Indra is bestowed with a heroic and almost brash and amorous character at times, even as his reputation and role diminished in later Hinduism with the rise of the Trimurti.

Indra is, with Varuna and Mitra, one of the Ādityas, the chief gods of the Rigveda (besides Agni and the others such as the Ashvins). He delights in drinking Soma, and the central Vedic myth is his heroic defeat of Vṛtrá, liberating the rivers, or alternatively, his smashing of the Vala cave, a stone enclosure where the Panis had imprisoned the cows that are habitually identified with Ushas, the dawn(s). He is the god of war, smashing the stone fortresses of the Dasyu, but he is also is invoked by combatants on both sides in the Battle of the Ten Kings.
Indra as depicted in Yakshagana, popular folk art of Karnataka

The Rig-Veda frequently refers to him as Śakra: the mighty-one. In the Vedic period, the number of gods was assumed to be thirty-three and Indra was their lord. (Some early post Rigvedic texts such as the Khilas and the late Vedic

Brihad-Aranyaka Upanishad enumerates the gods as the eight Vasus, the eleven Rudras, the twelve Adityas, Indra, and Prajapati). As lord of the Vasus, Indra was also referred to as Vāsava.

By the age of the Vedanta, Indra became the prototype for all lords and thus a king could be called Mānavendra (Indra or lord of men) and Rama, the hero of the Ramayana, was referred to as Rāghavendra (Indra of the clan of Raghu). Hence the original Indra was also referred to as Devendra (Indra of the Devas). However, Sakra and Vasava were used exclusively for the original Indra. Though modern texts usually adhere to the name Indra, the traditional Hindu texts (the Vedas, epics and Puranas) use Indra, Sakra and Vasava interchangeably and with the same frequency.

"Of the Vedas I am the Sama Veda; of the demigods I am Indra, the king of heaven; of the senses I am the mind; and in living beings I am the living force [consciousness]." (Bhagavad Gita 10.22)

In the Rig Veda, Indra is the king of the gods and ruler of the heavens. Indra is the god of thunder and rain and a great warrior, a symbol of courage and strength. He leads the Deva (the gods who form and maintain Heaven) and the elements, such as Agni (Fire), Varuna (Water) and Surya (Sun), and constantly wages war against the opponents of the gods, the demon-like Asuras. As the god of war, he is also regarded as one of the Guardians of the directions, representing the east. As the favourite 'national' god of the Vedic Indians, Indra has about 250 hymns dedicated to him in the Rigveda.

In Rig Veda, Indra the solar god is sometimes described as golden-bodied ("*Gora*" that means golden-yellowish) with golden jaw, nails, hair, beard.

One Atharva Vedic verse reads, "In Indra are set fast all forms of golden hue."

In the RV 1.65 reads, "SAKRA, who is the purifier (of his worshipers), and well-skilled in horses, who is wonderful and golden-bodied." Rig Veda also reads that Indra "is the dancing god who, clothed in perfumed garments, golden-cheeked rides his golden cart." One passage calls him both brown and yellow. "Him with the fleece they purify, brown, golden-hued, beloved of all, Who with exhilarating juice goes forth to all the deities"

Indra is described in the Rig Veda having blond, or 'yellow', hair. One part of the Rig Veda says, "At the swift draught the Soma-drinker waxed in might, the Iron One with yellow beard and yellow hair." The Rig Veda/Mandala 10/Hymn 96

In Hindu mythology, the rainbow is called Indra's Bow (Sanskrit: *indradhanus* इन्द्रधनुस्).

Chapter 9

Chinese and Japanese Mythology

China has over a billion people in its country today. China was united from a collection of independent cities around 2,000 years ago by an emperor named Yin Zheng (now called Qin Shi Huangdi). He tried to make the whole country uniform by having the people use the same money, measuring system, language and clothes. He made every one wear black clothes.

There are many different stories from ancient Chinese mythology. The dragon figure is prominent in Chinese lore. There are six seperate origin stories, a story of divine warfare between the gods, a flood myth, a catastrophe by fire, a drought myth and myths of gods handing down knowledge to the human race.

The following are 17 of the gods and goddesses of ancient China:

- Yu Huang Da Di- The Jade Emperor who was superior to all and attended to all the affairs of heaven. He organized the universe.
- Nuwa and Fuxi- Nuwa was part woman and dragon. Fuxi was part man and dragon. Nuwa became lonely and created humans. Fuxi was the first teacher. He taught humans how to survive.
- Sun Wukong was the God of Mischief. He was king of a band of monkeys. He caused so much trouble that a band was placed on his head to keep him in line.
- Guanyin is the Goddess of Mercy.
- Zhong Kui was the God of Healing.
- Niu Lang was called Ox Boy. He fell in love with the Goddess of Weaving, Zhi Nu.
- Guan Gong was the God of War
- Xi Wang Mu was the Goddess of Immortality.

- Lei Shen was the God of Thunder.
- Dian Mu was the Goddess of Lightning.
- Huang Di was the God of Law and Order.
- Cai Shen was the God of Wealth.
- Hong Shen was the God of the Southern Seas.
- Menshen are the Gods of Peaceful Sleep.

There are also many stories of emperors, sages and heroes. The story of the Eight Immortals is very interesting. The Eight Immortals are eight "Chinese" saints. They fight against evil and protect humans as they go on their journeys. Their names are as follows:

- Immortal Woman He (He Xiangu),
- Royal Uncle Cao (Cao Guojiu),
- Iron-Crutch Li (Tieguai Li),
- Lan Caihe,
- Lü Dongbin, leader;
- Philosopher Han Xiang (Han Xiang Zi),
- Elder Zhang Guo (Zhang Guo Lao), and
- Han Zhongli (Zhongli Quan).

There are many other ancient Chinese gods and goddesses and some of the names vary from source to source. There are other stories of Chinese folklore used to teach lessons in Chinese society. The Chinese god of longevity has a conehead, unlike the other Chinese Gods. Perhaps being the god of longevity, this is symbolic of what an elder race of gods, looked like.

Japanese:

The country or islands of Japan were unified about 1400 years ago under the Yamato Clan. Japan has a population of about 128 million people and is one of the most homogeneous countries in the world. The traditional religion of Japan is Shintoism. It involves the honoring of the ancestors. There are Shinto Priests and Priestessess which is a common thing for all older religions.

Shintoism involves the worship of Kami, or divine forces of nature. Shinto worshippers believe in the Kami of every thing. There are over 8 million gods and goddesses in the Japanese pantheon, but the major ancient gods and goddesses of Shintoism are as follows:

- Izanagi was the first god of the earth who created the world. He was the father of Amaterasu, Tsuki-yomi, and Susano.
- Izanami was the wife of Izanagi and the Goddess of the Earth.
- Kagu-Zuchi was the fire god. He was the last child of Izangi and Izanami.
- Amaterasu was the Sun Goddess and Ruler of Heaven.
- Tsuki-yomi was the God of the Moon and brother of Amatersau.
- Susano was the Storm God and brother of Amaterasu.
- Wakahiru-me was the younger sister of Amaterasu and Goddess of the Rising Sun.
- Kusa-nada-hime was the Rice Paddy Princess and wife of Susano.
- O-Kuni-Nushi was the God of Medicine and Sorcery and he was the son of Susano.
- Ame-no-Oshido-Mimi was the Son of Amaterasu who refused to go to Earth because it was too full of problems.
- Ninigi was the grandson of Amaterasu who finally went to Earth to reign.
- Kono-Hana-Sukuya-Himi was the daugher of a mountain god and wife of Ninigi.
- Takami-Musubi was one of Amaterasu's chief assistants.
- Amo-No-Uzume was a solar deity and Goddess of the Dawn.
- Inari was a Rice God and God of Prosperity.
- Ryujin was the God of the Ocean.

As with all mythologies, there are stories of heroes and wars and catastrophes. The emperors were of "royal blood" meaning they were descended from a god or goddess. In Japan, the royal family is descended from Amaterasu. The dragon is also a prominent figure in Japan. There also appears to be some connections between the Japanese Hata clan with the lost tribes of Israel and Christians.

Chapter 10

African Pantheons

According to Wikipedia:

The Mende people of Sierra Leone have their own secret societies that are segregated by gender. The Poro prepares men for leadership in the community, so they might attain wisdom, accept responsibility, and gain power. It begins with the child's grade of discovery, followed by extensive training and service. During the seven-year initiation period, the young men converse with each other using a secret language and password, known only to other Poro members. The member always knows and understands what is being said. This is part of the mystery of this secret society.

All Mende women when they reach puberty begin the initiation process into the *Sande* society. The goals of this secret society are to teach young Mende women the responsibilities of adulthood. The girls are taught to be hard working and modest in their behavior, especially towards their elders. Sande influences every aspect of a Mende woman's life; it is present before birth and still present after.

My Photo - Mende masks at the Milwaukee Museum of Art

The Dogon tribe of Mali, is a popular one due to their stories of gaining knowledge from gods and goddesses. Circumcism and other religious rites are practiced on both girls and boys.

An interesting goddess that is worshipped in West, Central, and Southern Africa, and in the Caribbean is Mami Wata. Mami Wata is a water spirit and is generally represented as a woman with a snake.

http://en.wikipedia.org/wiki/File:Mami_Wata_poster.png (public domain)

Mami Wata may appear as a mermaid, a man, or a woman. She is a mother goddess and her snake is a reference to being able to see the future. Mami Wata reminds me of Rhea.

Chapter 11

Polynesian and Aborigine Pantheons

Waimea Valley is one of the last partially intact native Hawaiian lands. It is called an Ahupua'a. The land consists of 1,800 acres of valley with botanical and ecological significance. There are many animals that roam freely in this preserved land.

My Photo

When I entered the preserve, I walked a trail and thought the area was only a nature preserve. But as I continued on the trail, to the right of me was a group of steps. I knew I had to step off the trail and follow these steps for some reason. As I walked up the steps and into a rocky area, I discovered a complete archaeological site. The area contained an ancient Hawaiian living site that belonged to a high priest and his family. The site included rock structures for housing animals, a rock structure for dead relatives, remains of a house for men and other remains.

My Photo

My Photo

My Photo

My Photo

I continued on and found a school house that was a reconstruction of a school for Hawaiian children. At the end of the trail, was a waterfall.

My Photo

My Photo

After turning around and heading back to the entrance of the valley, I found a temple that was partially reconstructed at the outside of the valley. It was an ancient temple dedicated to the God Lono, who was one of four primary deities. He was the god of agriculture, peace and music. The temple dates back to 1470 AD. I believe Lono is probably the god Dionysus-Osiris.

My Photo

My Photo

At Waikiki beach I found an ancient set of stones called *The Stones of Life*. These stones were said to be brought down for four healers who had travelled from other islands as far back as 400 AD. They were referred to as kahunas or wizards. They were skilled in the art of medicine and taught many healing ways to the people of O'ahu and other Hawaiian islands. They were said to be tall men but somewhat feminine and gentle. After healing and teaching healing ways, the kahunas said they would impart their power in one of the stones. After time, the stones were covered in sand, until they were rediscovered and uncovered and protected.

My Photo

A cave was used by the high chiefs of ancient days. I found it and then I entered Spirit Cave.

My Photo

The Polynesians include 1,000 islands scattered over the central and southern Pacific Ocean. Kanaloa was a Polynesian god of the underworld and of magic. From Wikepedia:

In the traditions of ancient Hawaii, Kanaloa is symbolized by the squid or by the octopus, and is typically associated with Kāne. It is also the name of an extinct volcano in Hawaiʻi.

In legends and chants Kāne and Kanaloa are portrayed as complementary powers (Beckwith 1970:62–65). For example: Kāne was called upon during the building of a canoe, Kanaloa during the sailing of it; Kāne governed the northern edge of the ecliptic, Kanaloa the southern; Kanaloa points to hidden springs, and Kāne then taps them out. In this way, they represent a divine duality of wild and taming forces like those observed (by Georges Dumézil, et al.) in Indo-European chief god-pairs like Odin–Týr and Mitra–Varuna, and like the popular yin and yang of Chinese Taoism.

Kanaloa is also considered to be the god of the Underworld and a teacher of magic. Legends state that he became the leader of the first group of spirits "spit out" by the gods. In time, he led them in a rebellion in which the spirits were defeated by the gods and as punishment were thrown in the Underworld.

However, depictions of Kanaloa as a god of evil, death, or the Underworld, in conflict with good deities like Kāne (a reading that contradicts Kanaloa and Kāne's paired invocations and shared devotees in Ancient Hawaii) are likely the result of European missionary efforts to recast the four major divinities of Hawaiʻi in the image of the Christian Trinity plus Satan. In traditional, pre-contact Hawaiʻi, it was Milu who was the god of the Underworld and death, not Kanaloa; the related Miru traditions of other Polynesian cultures confirms this.

The Eye of Kanaloa is an esoteric symbol associated with the god in New Age Huna teaching, consisting of a seven-pointed star surrounded by concentric circles that are regularly divided by eight lines radiating from the inner-most circle to the outer-most circle.

Kane and Kanaloa may refer to the same god and if it is, then it is Zeus. However, it makes more sense that Kanaloa is referring to Cronus and Kane is referring to Zeus. He may also be associated with the Maori god of the sea, Tangaro. From Wikipedia:

> **In Māori mythology, Tangaroa (also Takaroa) is one of the great gods, the god of the sea. He is a son of Ranginui and Papatuanuku, Sky and Earth. After he joins his brothers Rongo, Tūmatauenga, Haumia, and Tane in the forcible separation of their parents, he is attacked by his brother Tawhirimatea, the god of storms, and forced to hide in the sea. Tangaroa is the father of many sea creatures. Tangaroa's son, Punga, has two children, Ikatere, the ancestor of fish, and Tu-te-wehiwehi (or Tu-te-wanawana), the ancestor of reptiles. Terrified by Tawhirimatea's onslaught, the fish seek shelter in the sea, and the reptiles in the forests. Ever since, Tangaroa has held a grudge with Tāne, the god of forests, because he offers refuge to his runaway children (Grey 1971:1–5).**
>
> **Tagaloa is one of the oldest Polynesian deities and in western Polynesia (for example, Samoa and Tonga) traditions has the status of *supreme creator god*. In eastern Polynesian cultures Tangaroa is usually considered of equal status to Tāne and thus not supreme.**

A Kahuna is a Hawaiian name for a priest, sorcerer, magician, wizard, minister, expert in any profession. There are 40 different types of Kahunas. They range from experts in herbal healing to experts in boat making. The missionaries came to Hawaii and outlawed the Kahuna, but there is a revival of the Kahuna, today. The Kahuna communed with the ancient gods to help them in their crafts. Kahunas could be both male and female.

The Kohens are patriarchal priests of Jewish (Hebrew) lineage. According to Wikipedia:

> **The noun kohen is used in the Torah to refer to priests, both Jewish and non-Jewish, such as the Jewish nation as a whole, as well as the priests (Hebrew kohanim) of Baal (2Kings 10:19). During the existence of the Temple in Jerusalem, Kohanim performed the daily and holiday (Yom Tov) duties of sacrificial offerings.**

Kohanim sounds very similar to Kahuna. Christian priests are referred to as Komer in Hebrew. I have also seen pictures and stories of Tahitian temples that contained animal pens for pigs that were sacrificed to the gods of the temple. There are twenty-four different types of Kohens. Per Wikipedia:

> **King David assigned each of the 24 priestly clans to a weekly watch (Hebrew mishmeret) during which its members were responsible for maintaining the schedule of offerings at the Temple in Jerusalem (1Chronicles 24:3-5). This instated a cycle of 'priestly courses' or 'priestly divisions' which repeated itself roughly twice each year.**

So here again, is an eerie connection between two seemingly unrelated cultures.

Chapter 12

Nag Hammadi Library, Dead Sea Scrolls, and Book of Enoch

While looking for information on ancient writings, I stumbled into a set of ancient writings called the *Nag Hammadi Library*. This group of writings was discovered in Egypt in 1945. This library is apparently from the fourth century.

The library contains several new gospels that tell a different story of Jesus as well as human history. In the *Second Treatise of the Great Seth*, a less favorable view of the Ruling God and his Archons who created human bodies is given and the ruling God is referred to as the Evil Demiurge. This text talks about how the souls of Adam and Eve were captured into the fabricated bodies made by a group of Archons.

For Adam was a laughing stock, since he was made a counterfeit type of man by the Hebdomad, as if he had become stronger than I and my brothers. We are innocent with respect to him since we have not sinned. And Abraham and Isaac and Jacob were a laughingstock, since they, the counterfeit fathers, were given a name by the Hebdomad as if he had become stronger than I and my brothers. We are innocent with respect to him, since we have not sinned. David was laughingstock in that his son was named the Son of Man, having been influenced by the Hebdomad as if he had become stronger than I and the fellow members of my race. But we are innocent with respect to him; we have not sinned. Solomon was a laughingstock, since he thought that he was the Christ, having become vain through the Hebdomad, as if he had become stronger than I and my brothers. But we are innocent with respect to him. I have not sinned. The 12 prophets were laughingstocks, since they have come forth as imitations of the true prophets. They

came into being as counterfeits through the Hebdomad as if he had become stronger than I and my brothers. But we are innocent with respect to him, since we have not sinned. Moses, a faithful servant, was a laughingstock, having been named "the Friend" since they perversely bore witness concerning him who never knew me. Neither he nor those before him, from Adam to Moses and John the Baptist, none of them knew me nor my brothers.

For they had a doctrine of angels to observe dietary laws and bitter slavery, since they never knew truth, nor will they know it. For there is a great deception upon their soul making it impossible for them ever to find a Nous of freedom in order to know him, until they come to know the Son of Man. Now concerning my Father, I am he whom the world did not know, and because of this, it (the world) rose up against me and my brothers. But we are innocent with respect to him; we have not sinned.

For the Archon was a laughingstock because he said, "I am God, and there is none greater than I. I alone am the Father, the Lord and there is no other beside me. I am a jealous God who brings the sins of the fathers upon the children for three and four generations." As if he had become stronger than I and my brothers! But we are innocent with respect to him, in that we have not sinned, since we mastered his teaching. Thus he was in an empty glory. And he does not agree with our Father. And thus through our fellowship we grasped his teaching, since he was vain in an empty glory. And he does not agree with our Father, for he was a laughingstock and judgement and false prophecy.[36]

---

[36] James M. Robinson, *The Nag Hammadi Library* (New York:HarperSanFrancisco, 1988), 368-369.

The library talks about the Mother of God and appears to acknowledge the female and male aspects of the real God/creator. The library contains gospels from Peter, Mary the Magdalene, Thomas, Philip and James.

The Gospel of Thomas is quite interesting. It has several passages similar to what is in the four gospels of the Bible plus more.

> **Jesus said, "Do not give what is holy to dogs, lest they throw them on the dung heap. Do not throw the pearls [to] swine, lest they… it […]."**[37]
>
> **Jesus said, "Those here who do the will of my father are my brothers and my mother. It is they who will enter the kingdom of my father."**[38]
>
> **Simon Peter said to them, "Let Mary leave us, for women are not worthy of life."**
>
> **Jesus said, "I myself shall lead her in order to make her male, so that she too may become a living spirit resembling you males. For every woman who will make herself male will enter the kingdom of heaven."**[39]

The Hypostasis of the Archons speaks about how the chief ruler was cast into Tartaros and then sang praises to his mother and her daughter and was elevated to the 7th heaven.

> **This ruler, by being androgynous, made himself a vast realm, an extent without limit. And he contemplated creating offspring for himself, and created for himself seven offspring, androgynous just like their parent.**
>
> **And he said to his offspring, 'It is I who am the god of the entirety.' And**

---

[37] James M. Robinson, *The Nag Hammadi Library* (New York:HarperSanFrancisco, 1988), 136.

[38] James M. Robinson, *The Nag Hammadi Library* (New York:HarperSanFrancisco, 1988), 136-137.

[39] James M. Robinson, *The Nag Hammadi Library* (New York:HarperSanFrancisco, 1988), 138.

Zoe(Life), the daughter of Pistis Sophia, cried out and said to him, 'You are mistaken, Sakla!' for which the alternate name is Yaltabaoth. She breathed into his face, and her breath became a fiery angel for her; and that angel bound Yaldabaoth and cast him down into Tartaros, below the abyss.

Now when his offspring Sabaoth saw the force of that angel, he repented and condemned his father and his mother matter.
He loathed her, but he sang songs and praise up to Sophia and her daughter Zoe. And Sophia and Zoe caught him up and gave him charge of the seventh heaven, below the veil between above and below. And he is called 'God of the forces, Sabaoth,' since he is up above the forces of chaos, for Sophia established him.

Now when these (events) had come to pass, he made himself a huge four-faced chariot of cherubim and infinitely many angels to act as ministers, and also harps and lyres...

There I have taught you about the pattern of the rulers; and the matter in which it was expressed; and their parent; and their universe...

You, together with your offspring, are from the primeval father; from above, out of the imperishable light, their souls are come. Thus the authorities cannot approach them because of the spirit of truth present within them; and all who have become acquainted with this way exist deathless in the midst of dying mankind. Still that sown element (sperma) will not become known now....

He said to me, "Until the moment when the true man, within a modelled form, reveals the existence of (?)..[the spirit of] truth, which the father has sent.

Then he will teach them about everything: And he will anoint them with the ..unction of life eternal, given him from the undominated generation.

Then they will be freed of blind thought: And they will trample under foot death, which is of the authorities: And they will ascend into the limitless light, where this sown element belongs.

Then the authorities will relinquish their ages: And their angels will weep over their destruction: And their demons will lament their death.

Then all the children of the light will be truly acquainted with the truth and

> their root, and the father of entirety and the holy spirit: They will all say with a single voice, 'The father's truth is just, and the son presides over the entirely': And from everyone unto the ages of ages, 'Holy holy holy! Amen!'[40]

In the *On the Origin of the World* text, another recounting of how the Evil DemiUrge set up his throne is written:

> And before his mansion he created a throne, which was huge and was upon a four-faced chariot called "Cherubin." Now the Cherubin has eight shapes per each of the four corners, lion forms and calf forms and human forms and eagle forms, so that all the forms amount to sixty-four forms and (he created) seven archangels that stand before it; he is the eighth, and has authority. All the forms amount to seventy-two. Furthermore, from this chariot the seventy-two gods took shape; they took shape so that they might rule over the seventy-two languages of the peoples. And by the throne he created other, serpent-like angels, called "Saraphin", which praise him at all times.

> Thereafter he created a congregation (ekklesia) of angels, thousands and myriads, numberless, which resembled the congregation in the eighth heaven; and a firstborn called Israel-which is "the man that sees God"; and another being, called Jesus Christ, who resembles the savior above in the eighth heaven and who sits at his right upon a revered throne, and his left, there sits the virgin of the holy spirit, upon a throne and glorifying him. …Now where he sits is upon a throne of light (within a) great cloud that covers him. And there was no one with him in the cloud except Sophia <the daughter of> Pistis, instructing him about all the things that exist in the eighth heaven, so that the likenesses of those things might be created, in order that his reign might endure until the consummation of the heavens of chaos and their forces.[41]

---

[40] James M. Robinson, *The Nag Hammadi Library* (New York:HarperSanFrancisco, 1988), 168-169.

These writings seem to be describing the Cronus rebellion against Uranus and the Zeus rebellion against Cronus and the setting up of the Cronide kingdom.

---

[41] James M. Robinson, *The Nag Hammadi Library* (New York:HarperSanFrancisco, 1988), 176.

Chapter 13

Forbidden Texts

As part of my studies, I felt I had to read as many books as I could. I would read one book, which would lead me to a more obscure book and so forth. I stumbled into the Book of Enoch and then picked up a copy of the Dead Sea Scrolls, which also had some of Enoch's writings in it as well as a few other interesting tidbits. And then I hit the jackpot and stumbled into the Pseudipegrapha and some of the other lost books of the Bible such as the Book of Jasher and the Book of Tobit. All of these forbidden texts had one thing in common. They all pointed to a different view of Christianity than is being taught, today.

They also, go into extensive interaction of humans with angels and hierarchies and the structure of the hidden world that originated from the one invisible God. I will give some excerpts and summaries of these ancient forbidden texts in this chapter but highly recommend to those that yearn for the truth, to pick up some of these books and read them for yourself.

Enoch was a patriarch whose writings were considered to be heretical by the Catholic Church. A Jewish rabbi in the second century pronounced a curse on all those who had possession of it.[42] Most of Enoch's writings were confiscated and burned and people who possessed them were murdered as heretics. In 1773, a Scottish explorer by the name of James Bruce found a preserved copy of the book of Enoch in Ethiopia. James Bruce brought back 3 copies of the book with him. In 1821, Dr. Richard Laurence produced the first English translation of the texts.

The Dead Sea Scrolls were found in the 1940s and they contained some of Enoch's writings, also.

---

[42] Elizabeth Clare Prophet *Forbidden Mysteries of Enoch*(U.S.A.:Summit University Press, 1996), Page 8.

Enoch describes in detail, the inter-breeding of humans and the angels/watchers (as he called them). He describes in detail, who did it and how they were punished and that the inter-breeding of the humans and angels produced evil offspring who were giants.

Further, Enoch talks about how the angels taught the human females to wear jewelry and make-up to be more attractive and taught them about herbs.

Enoch travels through the different heavens and meets the "Lord" and then meets "God". The following are passages from the book of Enoch.

It happened after the sons of men had multiplied in those days, that daughters were born to them, elegant and beautiful.

And when the angels, the sons of heaven, beheld them, they became enamored of them, saying to each other, Come, let us select for ourselves wives from the progeny of men, and let us beget children.

Then their leader Samyaza said to them; I fear that you may perhaps be indisposed to the performance of this enterprise;

And I alone shall suffer for so grievous a crime.
But they answered him and said; We all swear;

And bind ourselves by mutual execrations, that we will not change our intention, but execute our projected undertaking.

Then they swore all together, and all bound themselves by mutual execrations. Their whole number was two hundred, who descended upon Ardis, which is the top of mount Armon.

That mountain therefore was called Armon, because they had sworn upon it,

    and bound themselves by mutual execrations.

    These are their names of their chiefs: Samyaza, who was their leader, Urakabarameel, Akibeel, Tamiel, Ramuel, Danel, Azkeel, Saraknyal, Asael, Armers, Batraal, Anane, Zavebe, Samsaveel, Ertael, Turel, Yomyael, Arazyal. These were their perfects of the two hundred angels, and the remainder were all with them.

    Then they took wives, each choosing for himself; whom they began to approach, and with whom they cohabited; teaching them sorcery, incantations, and the dividing of roots and trees.

    And the women conceiving brought forth giants.
    Whose stature was each three hundred cubits.

    These devoured all which the labour of men produced; until it became impossible to feed them;

    When they turned themselves against men, in order to devour them;
    And began to injure birds, beasts, reptiles and fishes, to eat their flesh one after another, and to drink their blood.
    Then the earth reproved the unrighteous.[43]

The angels taught their children how to make swords, knives and breastplates and how to use them for war.

    Moreover Azazyel taught men to make swords, knives, shields, breastplates, the fabrication of mirrors, and the workmanship of bracelets and ornaments, the use of paint, the beautifying of the eyebrows, the use of stones of every valuable and select kind, and of all sorts of dyes, so that the world became altered.

---

[43] Elizabeth Clare Prophet *Forbidden Mysteries of Enoch* (U.S.A.:Summit University Press, 1996), 92-94.

Impiety increased; fornication multiplied; and they transgressed and corrupted all their ways.

Amazarak taught all the sorceries, and dividers or roots;

Armers taught the solution of sorcery;

Barkayal taught the observers of the stars;

Akibeel taught signs;

Tamiel taught astronomy;

And Asaradel taught the motion of the moon.

And men, being destroyed, cried out; and their voice reached to heaven.[44]

The people cry out against the atrocities committed by the offspring of the angels. Enoch is taken up by God(?) to testify against these angels and then remains in protective custody with God. The Most High Lord orders Raphael to bind the leader of the angels who came down, Azazyel, hand and foot. Gabriel is sent to destroy the offspring of the Angels by inciting them to destroy each other. Michael binds Samyaza and his offspring for 70 generations underneath the earth. The flood is sent to destroy the children of the angels.

Then Michael and Gabriel, Raphael, Suryal, and Uriel, looked down from heaven, and saw the quantity of blood which was shed on earth, and all the iniquity which was done upon it, and said one to another, It is the voice of their cries;

The earth deprived of her children has cried even to the gate of heaven.

And now to you, O ye holy ones of heaven, the souls of men complain, saying, Obtain Justice for us with the Most High. Then they said to their Lord, the King, Thou art Lord of lords, God of gods, King of kings. The throne of thy glory is forever and ever, and forever and ever is thy name sanctified and glorified....

Then the Most High, the Great and Holy One spoke,

And sent Arsayalalyur to the son of Lamech,

---

[44] Elizabeth Clare Prophet *Forbidden Mysteries of Enoch*(U.S.A.:Summit University Press, 1996), 94-95.

Saying, Say to him in my name, Conceal thyself.

Then explain to him the consummation which is about to take place; for all the earth shall perish;

the waters of a deluge shall come over the whole earth, and all things which are in it shall be destroyed.

And now teach him how he may escape, and how his seed may remain in all the earth.

Again the Lord said to Raphael, Bind Azazyel hand and foot; cast him into darkness; and opening the desert which is in Dudael, cast him in there.

Throw upon him hurled and pointed stones, covering him with darkness.

There shall he remain forever; cover his face, that he may not see the light.

And in the great day of judgment let him be cast into the fire.

Restore the earth, which the angels have corrupted; and announce life to it, that I may revive it…

To Gabriel also the Lord said, Go to the biters, to the reprobates, to the children of fornication; and destroy the children of fornication, the offspring of the Watchers, from among men; bring them forth, and excite them one against another. Let them perish by mutual slaughter; for length of days shall not be theirs.

They shall all entreat thee, but their fathers shall not obtain their wishes respecting them; for they shall hope for eternal life, and that they may live, each of them, five hundred years…

Purify the earth from all oppression, from all injustice, from all crime, from all impiety, and from all the pollution which is committed upon it. Exterminate them from the earth.

Then shall all the children of men be righteous, and all nations shall pay me divine honors, and bless me; and all shall adore me….

Before all these things Enoch was concealed; nor did any one of the sons of men know where he was concealed, where he had been, and what had happened.

> **He was wholly engaged with the holy ones, and with the Watchers in his days.**
>
> **I, Enoch, was blessing the great Lord and King of peace.**
>
> **And behold the Watchers called me Enoch the scribe.**
>
> **Then the Lord said to me: Enoch, scribe of righteousness, go tell the Watchers of heaven, who have deserted the lofty sky, and their holy everlasting station, who have been polluted with women.**
>
> **And have done as the sons of men do, by taking to themselves wives, and who have been greatly corrupted on the earth;**
>
> **That on the earth they shall never obtain peace and remission of sin. For they shall not rejoice in their offspring; they shall behold the slaughter of their beloved; shall lament for the destruction of their sons; and shall petition forever; but shall not obtain mercy and peace.**[45]

It is important to note, that even after the flood, the giants reappear. This sounds again like the first rebellion of Cronus against Uranus.

The Dead Sea Scrolls have some more writings from Enoch. In *Tales of the Patriarchs*, Lamech calls for his father, Methuselah to ask his father Enoch, to ask him if his son, Noah is really his son because of the appearance of Noah (possibly albino). Methuselah finds Enoch with the Holy Ones on a mountain and confirms with him that Noah is Lamech's son and then Enoch tells him what will happen to Noah. Methuselah tells Lamech this and Lamech is then convinced.

> **Then I decided that the conception was at the hands of Watchers, that the seed had been planted by Holy Ones or Nephil[im]… I was in a turmoil because of this infant. Then I, Lamech, hurriedly went to [my] wi[fe], Bitenosh,[and I said to her,] ["I adjure you by…] and by the Most High, by the Lord, the Great One, by the King of all Et[eternity… have you conceived] [by one of] the Sons of Heaven? Tell**

---

[45] Elizabeth Clare Prophet *Forbidden Mysteries of Enoch*(U.S.A.:Summit University Press, 1996), 94-95.

me every detail truthfully [...] [in truth] make it known to me, without lies. Was this [...?] by the King of Eternity. You are to speak with me in utter truth, without lies [...]."

Then Bitenosh, my wife, replied to me very passionately, wee[ping...]. She said, "O, my brother, my lord, remember my voluptuousness [...] before the time of lovemaking, and my ardent response. I [am telling you] the whol[e] truth [...] and my mind was then changed. Now when my wife Bitenosh saw that my disposition had changed, [...] Then she restrained her anger, speaking with me and saying, "O, my lord, my [brother, remember...] my pleasure. I swear to you by the Great Holy One, by the King of He[aven...] that this seed comes from you, this conception was by you, the planting of [this] fruit is yours [..It was] not by any stranger, neither by any of the Watchers, nor yet by any Sons of Heav[en. Why has] your expression been so altered, your mood so depressed? [...] Surely I am speaking with you truthfully.[46]

Notice Lamech's wife refers to him as her brother as well as her husband. This chapter continues on with the story of Abraham and Sara. The story starts with a dream Abraham had regarding men wanting to kill him when he and Sarah enter Egypt. Sarah interprets the dream and knows she has to refer to Abraham as her brother when they go to Egypt. When the two do go to Egypt, Sarah is taken by the pharaoh because of her beauty and Abraham's life is spared because she refers to him as her brother.

Abraham prays for retribution and his God sends an affliction to the Pharaoh and all the men in his house. As a result, none of the men are able to perform sexually and the Pharaoh can't have sex with Sarah even though he has kept her for two years.

Finally, the Pharaoh finds out that Sarah was Abraham's wife and releases her to Abraham and asks him to pray for the afflictions to be removed from his household. Abraham does so and the afflictions are removed.

---

[46] Michael Wise, Martin Abegg, Jr., & Edward cook, The Dead Sea Scrolls (New York: HarperSanfranciso, 1996), 76.

The *Book of Enoch* was found among the Dead Sea Scrolls and has included all but one of the five Ethiopian versions of the *Book of Enoch*. The *Book of Giants* was part of the Dead Sea Scrolls and again talks about the offspring of the angels and human women. Although some of the fragments of the chapter are missing, there appears to be a passage referring to how the angels tried to also procreate with animals as well as with humans.

> **[.. two hundred] donkeys, two hundred asses, two hundred… rams of the] flock, two hundred goats, two hundred […beast of the] field from every animal, from every [bird…][…] for miscegenation […].[47]**

There is also mention of Gilgamesh in this chapter.

> **'concerns the death of our souls […] and all his comrades, [and Oh]ya told them what Gilgamesh said to him […] and it was said […]"concerning […] the leader has cursed the potentates" and the giants were glad at his words. Then he turned and left […][48]**

---

[47] Michael Wise, Martin Abegg, Jr., & Edward cook, The Dead Sea Scrolls (New York: HarperSanfranciso, 1996), 247.

[48] Michael Wise, Martin Abegg, Jr., & Edward cook, The Dead Sea Scrolls (New York: HarperSanfranciso, 1996), 249.

Chapter 14

Giants and Little People Everywhere

As with the Little People, the giant red-haired people have been all over the Earth and probably exist in one form or another, today.

There are several mummies and skeletons being found that don't fit the mold for what is thought to be an ancient Native American. Specifically the following sites contained these anomalies:

Windover Bog Mummies in Florida

Spirit Cave Man in Fallon, Nevada

The Sitecah of Lovelock Cave in Nevada

Kenniwick Man of Washington State

Mention of Giant Skeletons found all over the Midwest (Wisconsin, Illinois, Ohio, and so on.)

The Princess at Aztalan

Red-Haired Mummies of Peru

Lovelock Cave Mummies

It is a touchy subject as to the true origins of these ancient people; however, the truth must come out. There are those such as myself that believe that Europeans travelled across the

Atlantic Ocean and populated the Americas atleast 10,000 years ago and probably well before that. Tales of St. Brendan and Viking travels to America help to corroborate this theory.

What I find interesting is the intense pressure to prevent DNA testing of these finds or the fact that many of the remains that were turned over to museums have simply disappeared. This is also the case for any finds of The Little People mummies from out west in America. In the specific case of the Lovelock Cave mummies of Nevada, it is cited in wikipedia that a fraternity got a hold of a red-haired mummy from the cave and actually boiled it as part of an initiation ceremony in 1911. How in the world was this allowed to happen? Unfortunately, many mummies from Egypt were treated in a terrible manner as well and mummy unwrapping parties took place in the 1800s as well as the using of the mummies for fake medicinals. According to an article on Wikipedia the following is written about Lovelock Cave.

> **According to Paiute oral history, the Si-Te-Cah are a legendary tribe whose mummified remains were discovered (under four feet of guano) by miners in what is now known as "Lovelock Cave" in Lovelock, Nevada, United States. Although the cave had been mined since 1911, it was not until 1912 when miners notified authorities. An archeological excavation ensued producing 10,000 artifacts. "Si-Te-Cah" literally means "tule-eaters" in the language of the Paiute Indians. Tule is a fibrous water plant. In order to escape harassment from the Paiutes, the Si-Te-Cahs were said to have lived on rafts made of tule on the lake.**

> **According to the Paiutes, the Si-Te-Cah were a hostile and warlike tribe who practiced cannibalism. The Si-Te-Cah and the Paiutes were at war, and after a long struggle a coalition of tribes trapped the remaining Si-Te-Cah in Lovelock Cave. When they refused to come out, the Indians piled brush before the cave mouth and set it aflame. The Si-Te-Cah were annihilated.**

> **A written report by James H. Hart, the first of two miners to excavate the cave in the fall of 1911, recalls that in the north-central part of the cave, about four feet**

deep, "was a striking looking body of a man "six feet six inches tall." His body was mummified and his hair distinctly red." (Loud & Harrington, page 87). Unfortunately in the first year of mining, some of the human remains and artifacts were lost and destroyed. "The best specimen of the adult mummies was boiled and destroyed by a local fraternal lodge, which wanted the skeleton for initiation purposes." (Loud & Harrington, page 5). Also, several of the fiber sandals found in the cave were remarkably large, and one reported at over 15 inches (38 cm) in length was said to be on display at the Nevada Historical Society's museum in Reno in 1952.

I find the story of the fraternity's destruction of the mummy, even more suspicious. It was as if the evidence of a giant race of red-haired people that dominated in the past, was being purposely suppressed. We must press on for the truth. According to wikipedia:

The Spirit Cave mummy is the oldest human mummy found in North America. It was discovered in 1940 in Spirit Cave, thirteen miles east[1] of Fallon, Nevada by the husband-and-wife archaeological team of Sydney and Georgia Wheeler.

The Wheelers, working for the Nevada State Parks Commission, were surveying possible archaeological sites to prevent their loss due to guano mining. Upon entering Spirit Cave they discovered the remains of two people wrapped in tule matting. One set of remains, buried deeper than the other, had been partially mummified (the head and right shoulder). The Wheelers, with the assistance of local residents, recovered a total of sixty-seven artifacts from the cave.

These artifacts were examined at the Nevada State Museum where they were estimated to be between 1,500 and 2,000 years old. They were deposited at the Nevada State Museum's storage facility in Carson City where they remained for the next fifty-four years

In 1996 University of California, Riverside anthropologist R. Ervi Taylor examined seventeen of the Spirit Cave artifacts using mass spectrometry. The results indicated that the mummy was approximately 9,400 years old (uncalibrated Radio-Carbon Years Before-Present (RCYBP); ~11.5 Kya calibrated) — older than any previously known North American mummy.

In March 1997, the Paiute-Shoshone Tribe of the Fallon Reservation and Colony made a Native American Graves Protection and Repatriation Act (NAGPRA) claim of cultural affiliation with the artifacts.

Further study determined that the mummy exhibits Caucasoid characteristics resembling the Ainu, although a definitive affiliation has not been established. There is also a possible link to Polynesians and Australians that is stronger than to any Native American culture.

There is mention of the Giants in the Dead Sea Scrolls and the Pseudipigrapha's 3rd Book of Baruch.

As you can see, the story of red-haired giants is global. The fairy people of New Zealand were said to be Caucasoid as well. They even created a stamp showing a somewhat albino being as being the New Zealand fairy.

Chapter 15

Mounds, Effigies, Megalithic Structures,
Human Origins, and World Catastrophies

Diodorus Siculus wrote about the origins of humans in his *Library of History*.

Now the first men, since none of the things useful for life had yet been discovered, led a wretched existence, having no clothing to cover them, knowing not the use of dwelling and fire, and also being totally ignorant of cultivated food. For since they also even neglected the harvesting of the wild food, they laid by no store of its fruits against their needs; consequently large numbers of them perished in the winters because of the cold and the lack of food. Little by little, however, experience taught them both to take to the caves in winter and to store such fruits as could be preserved. And when they had become acquainted with fire and other useful things, the arts also and whatever else is capable of furthering man's social life were gradually discovered. Indeed, speaking generally, in all things it was necessity itself that became man's teacher, supplying in appropriate fashing instruction in every matter to a creature which was well endowed by nature and had, as its assistants for eery purpose, hands and speech and sagacity of mind. [49]

As I have said before, all megalith structures were used as calendars and used for ceremonial purposes. Many times, the mounds included burials, but also aligned to catch the sun rays during equinoxes or solstices. Every culture around the world has their story of various time periods, multiple races of men, stories of giants and little people, and castrophes. The Mayan Popul Vuh mentions five suns/ castrophes. All of the stories are the same. There have

---

[49] Diodorus Siculus, *The Library of History Volume 1*, page 31.

been extinctions of previous races due to natural diasters, wars, and exterminations and starvations. All talk of a group of gods/goddesses who gave them civilization and laws.

It is my belief that the similarity of all ancient structures comes from the global journeys of this ancient family of Zeus and his descendants.

Chapter 16

Modern Religion, Alice Bailey, and Mystery Cults

I've come across material that shows that Jesus survived the crucifixion and may have been in a state similar to a coma or state that the Yogis put themselves into, when he was removed from the cross. He may have been nurtured back to health and may have traveled across the Middle East, with the assumed name, Yuz Asaf, with his mother and a few disciples and ended up living in India.

The book, *Jesus Lived In India,* by Holger Kersten sites the current tomb of Jesus in Kashmir and the tomb of Mary in Pakistan. Holger starts out with the true story of a Russian historian, Nicolai Notovitch who traveled to the Ladakh region of Kashmir where he met a Buddhist lama who told him the story of their son of God whom they call Prophet Issa. After talking to this lama, Nicolai realized they were referring to Jesus Christ. Nicolai wrote a book about what he found, but it was not well received.

The Buddhists believe Jesus was a bodhisattva and that he's coming again through reincarnation. This information has been squelched in the Western world by the church.

His mother, Mary, appears to have been buried in Mari, Pakistan. Through all my readings of ancient religious texts, they continually repeat the theme that there is no room for flesh in the higher spiritual realms. The body is left behind in the world of the physical.

I've also read that Moses appears to be buried in India, too. Isn't this interesting? What would the churches do if this information was proven and disseminated all over the world? To give you an idea of what they might do, one must look back at the strange circumstances surrounding the death of John Paul I. He was 66 years old when he became Pope and was in good health. He mysteriously died about one month after taking office (August 26 to September 28, 1978). His body was embalmed and then cremated. Cremation went against Catholic teachings at the time. There is a theory that he was murdered by the senate of cardinals through poisoning because he openly supported women's rights and stated in one of his earlier speeches that God was not only the Heavenly Father but the Heavenly Mother, too.[50] He was also going to support artificial birth control and look into allegations of a link between the Vatican bank and the Mafia. One of the cardinals that he asked to look into the mafia connection, Cardinal Jean Villot, died within six months of these events. It's clear that something strange was going on and it's even stranger how the press has ignored what was going on and even stranger that Catholics didn't question what had happened to their Pope.

The writings of Alice Bailey are even more disturbing. She describes the plans of the global elite to decrease the human population, control natural resources through corporations, control and breed the general population through a group of scientists and have the elites live extended lives of comfort while the United Nations becomes the world government.

Most secret societies have elements of Judaism and Islamic symbolism as well as Egyptian. They are simply old boy's clubs used to manipulate the world for the elites.

Those involved with the occult believe they have power by following strict rituals. The occult and other world is a vast subject for another day.

In conclusion, I have shown you the ancient writings that tell you exactly where all ancient mythologies and modern day religions come from. When using comparative mythology and using the writings of the ancient past, the story of Zeus and his bloodline can be pieced together. Father Zeus wanted a better world and for a time he and his family made things better. Unfortunately, the world is at the edge of a castrophe that will be made by men who feel they are better than all of the human race and they gained power through lies, murder, war, and absolute treachery. It's time for a dose of the truth and an end to this out of control train of lies and destruction. It's time to go back to the ways that were given to us all without priests or elites and back to the true ways of Father Zeus, Mother Goddess Rhea, and all of the teachings from the Cronide line. Eat, drink, be merry and harm ye none and take care of your family and each other.

---

[50] John Van Auken, *The End Times* (Virginia, ARE Press, 1994), 119.

Bibliography

Bailey, Alice. <u>Initiation Human and Solar.</u> New York: Classic Books International, 2010.

Bailey, Alice. <u>Discipleship In the New Age II.</u> New York: Lucis Publishing Company, 1955.

Bailey, Alice. <u>The Externalisation of the Hierachy.</u> New York: Lucis Publishing Company, 1957.

Bailey, Alice. <u>A Treatise on White Magic.</u> New York: Lucis Publishing Company, 1951.

Bailey, Alice. <u>Eduction In The New Age.</u> New York: Lucis Publishing Company, 1954.

Bailey, Alice. <u>The Reappearance of The Christ.</u> New York: Lucis Publishing Company, 1948.

Bailey, Alice. <u>The Destiny of The Nations.</u> New York: Lucis Publishing Company, 1949.

Bailey, Foster. <u>Running God's Plan.</u> New York: Lucis Publishing Company, 1972.

Bailey, Foster. <u>Changing Esoteric Values.</u> New York: Lucis Publishing Company, 1954.

Bailey, Foster. <u>The Spirit of Masonry.</u> New York: Lucis Publishing Company, 1957.

Beck, Walter. Dogon Africa's People of the Cliffs. New York: Harry N Abrams, 2000.

Bellows, Henry Adams. The Poetic Edda. New York: Dover Publications, 2004.

Campanelli, Pauline. Ancient Ways Reclaiming Pagan Traditions. MN: Llewellyn Publications, 1998.

Cayce, Edgar Evans. *Edgar Cayce on Atlantis.* New York: Warner Books, Inc., 1968.

Charlesworth, James H.. *The Old Testament Pseudepigrapha Volume 1.* New York: Doubleday, 1983.

Charlesworth, James H.. *The Old Testament Pseudepigrapha Volume 2.* New York: Doubleday, 1985.

Clayton, Peter. Chronicle of the Pharaohs North India Experience Variances. To the Himalayas. Lonely Planet, 1995.

Current, Richard Nelson. Wisconsin A History. Urbana and Chicago: University of Illinois Press, 1977.

D'Aulaire's Ingri and Edgar Parin. Book of Greek Myths. U.S.A.: Delacorte Press, 1962.

Dalley, Stephanie. *Myths From Mesopotamia.* Oxford: Oxford University Press, 1989.

Dames, Michael. Ireland A Sacred Journey. Boston: Element, 2000.

Exploring Egypt and the Red Sea. The Land of Antiquities. SB Productions, 2003.

Evans Lady Hestia. Mythology The Gods, Heroes, and Monsters of Ancient Greece. Cambridge, Massachusetts: Candlewick Press, 2007.

Erdoes, Richard and Alfonso Ortiz. American Indian Myths and Legends. New York: Pantheon Books, 1984.

Fritz, Jean. Brendan the Navigator. New York: Penguin Putnam Books, 1979.

Garniner, Alan H., The Royal Canon of Turin, Oxford: Griffith Institute, 1997.

Gardner, Laurence. *Genesis of the Grail Kings.* USA: Element Books, 2000.

Harris, Geraldine. Gods & Pharaohs. New York: Peter Bedrick Books, 1981.

Hornung, Erik. *Akhenaten and the Religion of Light.* London: Cornell University Press, 1995.

Holy Bible The New Revised Standard Version with Apocrypha. Nashville, Tennessee: Thomas Nelson, Inc., 1990.

Hall, Robert L.. An Archaeology of the Soul, Chicago: University of Illiois Press, 1997.

Hall, Mark. Thunderbirds America's Living Legends of Giant Birds. New York: Paraview Press, 2004.

Haywood, John. Atlas of the Celtic World. London: Thames and Hudson, LTD, 2001.

Irish American Heritage. American Cultures for Children. Schlessinger Media, 1997.

Joeseph, Frank. Atlantis in Wisconsin. Lakeville, MN: Galde Press Inc., 1998.

Kummer, Patricia. Enchantment of the World, Tibet. Children's Press Scholastic Inc., 2003.

Kevin Eyres. The Secrets of Ireland. New York: Barnes and Noble, 2006.

Kersten, Holger. *Jesus Lived in India.* U.S.A. and Australia: Element Books, 1999.

Kerenyi, Carl. Dionysus Archetypal Image of Indestructible Life. New Jersey: Princetown University Press, 1976.

Kramer, Samuel Noah. *The Sumerians Their History, Culture, and Character.* Chicago & London: The University of Chicago Press, 1963.

Lindow, John. Norse Mythology. New York: Oxford University Press, 2001.

Lonely Planet West Africa, Benin, Mali and Burkina Faso. Lonely Planet, 1996.

Loew Patty. Indian Nations of Wisconsin. Madison, WI: Wisconsin Historical Society Press, 2001.

Murphy, Anthony and Richard Moore. Island of the Setting Sun. In Search of Ireland's Ancient Astronomers. Spain: Graticas Cems, 2006.

Nelson, Stephanie. Hesiod Theogony and Work and Days, New England: Boston University, 2009.

Nies, Judith. Native American History. New York: Ballantine Books, 1996.

Nonnos. Dionysiaca. Massachusetts: Harvard University Press, 1984.

O'Brien, Jacqueline and Peter Harbison. Ancient Ireland. New York: Oxford Press, 1996.

Paola, Tomie De. Fin M'Coul The Giant of Knockmany Hill. New York: Scholastic, 1981.

Plutarch, Moralia, London: Harvard University Press, 1936.

Prophet, Elizabeth Clare. Forbidden Mysteries of Enoch. U.S.A.: Summit University Press, 1996.

Randall, Ronne. The Children's Book of Myths and Legends. New York: Barnes & Noble, 2001.

Robinson, James M.. *The Nag Hammadi Library.* U.S.A.: HarperSanFrancisco, 1988.

Siculus, Diodorus. Library of History Books London: Harvard Univerty Press, 1968.

Sheinkin, David. *Path of the Kabbalah.* New York: Paragon House, 1986.

Sutton, Antony. *America's Secret Establishment.* Montana: Liberty House Press, 1986.

Scarre, Chris. Exploring Prehistoric Europe. New York: Oxford University Press, 1998.

Smith, David Lee. Folklore of the Winnebago Tribe. Norman and London: University of Oklahoma Press, 1997.

Streissguth, Thomas. Life in Ancient Egypt. San Diego, CA: Lucent Books, 2001.

Scranton, Laird. The Science of the Dogon. Vermont: Inner Traditions, 2006.

Sharp, Ann Wallace. Indigeneous People of the World Australia. San Diego, CA: Lucent Books, 2003.

Westwell, Ian. Timeless India. London: Compendium Publishing, 2007.

Walker, Henry John. Valerius Maximus Memorable Deeds and Sayings. Indianapolis: Hackett Pubishing Company, 2004.

White, Ellen. Great Controversy. Florida: Laymen for Religious Liberty, Inc., 1990.

Van Auken, John. *The End Times*. Virginia Beach: ARE Press, 1994.

Wise, Michael, Martin Abegg, Jr., & Edward Cook. *The Dead Sea Scrolls*. U.S.A.: HarperSanFrancisco, 1996.

Woodward, Susan L and Jerry N. McDonald. *Indian Mounds of the Middle Ohio Valley.* Blacksburg, Virginia: The McDonald & Woodward Publishing Company, 1999.

Waddell, W.G.. <u>Manetho</u>, London: Harvard University Press, 2004.

Wikipedia

Zell-Ravenheart, Oberon and the Grey Council. <u>Grimoire for the Apprentice Wizard.</u> NJ: New Page Books, 2004.

Made in the USA
Columbia, SC
31 March 2021